The Ends of the World

To Irene, a Terran of the world to come

The Ends of the World

Déborah Danowski and
Eduardo Viveiros de Castro

Translated by Rodrigo Nunes

polity

First published in Portuguese as *Há mundo por vir? Ensaio sobre os medos e os fins*,
© Déborah Danowski and Eduardo Viveiros de Castro, 2014 (revised edition 2015)

This English edition © Polity Press, 2017

10

Obra publicada com o apoio do Ministério da Cultura do Brasil / Fundação Biblioteca
Nacional

This work was published with the support of the Ministry of Culture of Brazil / National
Library Foundation

MINISTÉRIO DA CULTURA
Fundação BIBLIOTECA NACIONAL

Polity Press
65 Bridge Street
Cambridge CB2 1UR, UK

Polity Press
350 Main Street
Malden, MA 02148, USA

ISBN-13: 978-1-5095-0397-1
ISBN-13: 978-1-5095-0398-8 (pb)

A catalogue record for this book is available from the British Library.

Names: Danowski, Déborah, author. | Castro, Eduardo Batalha Viveiros de, author.
Title: The ends of the world / Déborah Danowski, Eduardo Viveiros de Castro Other
  titles: Há mundo por vir? English
Description: Malden, MA : Polity, 2016. | Translation of: Há mundo por vir? | Includes
  bibliographical references and index.
Identifiers: LCCN 2016017844 (print) | LCCN 2016031811 (ebook) | ISBN
  9781509503971 (hardback) | ISBN 1509503978 (hardcover) | ISBN 9781509503988
  (paperback) | ISBN 9781509504008 (mobi) | ISBN 9781509504015 (epub)
Subjects: LCSH: End of the world–Philosophy. | Metaphysics–Philosophy. | Fear–
  Philosophy. | BISAC: SOCIAL SCIENCE / Anthropology / Cultural.
Classification: LCC BL503 .D3613 2016 (print) | LCC BL503 (ebook) | DDC 001.9–dc23
LC record available at https://lccn.loc.gov/2016017844

Typeset in 10.5 on 12 pt Sabon
by Toppan Best-set Premedia Limited
Printed and bound in Great Britain by TJ Books Limited, Padstow

For further information on Polity, visit our website: politybooks.com

Contents

Foreword by Bruno Latour

What Isabelle Stengers calls *the intrusion of Gaia* is something that makes us lose all our bearings. Yes, Gaia is an intruder in the sense that nothing had been prepared, thought, planned, predicted, instituted for life under its sign. Nothing, at least, during that historical period which we can no longer call modernity. There was Nature, to be sure, that cold, eternal, distant figure which could dictate its laws to all human actions – including economic law. But this deity strikes us today as too outdated, too naive in its anthropocentrism. In any case, it too was eventually secularized. How can we then become familiar with Gaia, the intruder? This is where the two authors of this essay in mythocosmology step in: an anthropologist with philosophical leanings, a philosopher with an ecological bent. And they do not start from the beginning, of course (as if one had to go from the Big Bang, via Lucy, Lascaux, and so on, to get to the ecological crisis), but from the only place from which it is possible to start, namely, the end. Not the end of times, like Saint John, but the *suspension* of the ways in which time used to pass. The essay sallies forth in an inventory-like manner, a guided tour across the cabinet of curiosities of present philosophical and literary monstrosities, some of them quite fashionable, others not as well known, but all of them symptomatic of the present state of alarm. It then moves on to anthropology, to those indigenous worlds that never needed to give themselves either a Nature or a Culture. The tone changes because the worlds change. Finally, it is necessary to go into politics. It is with politics and through it that the book draws to an end, evoking the febrile mobilization of all collectives that know that time is no longer on their side. And thus it all starts again – or will start, leaving behind much of what we had grown used to believing in. This book must be read the way one takes a cold shower. So we get used to it. So we prepare. Expecting the worst.

But if we, who are kings of nature, shall have no fear, who shall?

Clarice Lispector

Unlike us, white people are not afraid of being crushed by the falling sky. But one day they may fear that as much as we do!

Davi Kopenawa

Prefatory note

"Things are changing so fast that it is hard to keep track," says Bruno Latour in a text that we cite right at the start of this book's second chapter. This applies perfectly to *The Ends of the World*. The book that now stands before the reader's eyes is the translation of the Portuguese edition, published in October 2014 by Cultura e Barbárie and Instituto Socioambiental, under the title *Há Mundo Por Vir? Ensaio sobre os medos e os fins*.[1] Since then, the stubborn march of global warming, on the one hand, and the ever growing accumulation of discourses (in the broad sense) on the "end of the world" and the Anthropocene, as well as the cloud of themes that the latter term so conveniently and polemically summarizes, on the other hand, has been of such magnitude that any attempt to update the arguments formulated only a couple of years ago would be a nigh impossible task. Let us just recall a few important milestones that have since occurred, which would no doubt impact various passages of this book: the international colloquium, "The Thousand Names of Gaia: From the Anthropocene to the Age of the Earth" (Rio de Janeiro, September 2014), organized by the two authors of *The Ends of the World*, among others, and bringing together several fundamental thinkers working on its subject; the appearance of the papal encyclical *Laudato Si'*, which marked the Vatican's properly spectacular entrance in the debate; the apparition (we choose the word advisedly) of *An Ecomodernist Manifesto*, a document whose production was led by the Breakthrough Institute and which was undersigned by many a pro-capitalist celebrity, radicalizing even further the positions defended by that think tank which this book discusses; various texts engaging with *Laudato Si'* as well as many others lambasting *An Ecomodernist Manifesto*, some of which were penned by authors also discussed in our book; the publication of Jason Moore's *Capitalism in the Web of Life: Ecology and the Accumulation of Capital*, which develops an exhaustive narrative of a historical materialist bent on the Anthropocene (rechristened "Capitalocene"); the veritable explosion of events, texts, and manifestos of the "accelerationist" current, which seems to have come of age somewhat – an impression reinforced by the way in which water has progressively been added to its originally thick Promethean wine; and, it goes without saying, the Paris Agreement, a document produced at the COP21 that took place in December 2015, a conference which, perhaps more than any of the other previous 20, managed to instill in environmentalists and scientists an equal combination of hope and disappointment, by dint of managing to produce a consensus among members regarding the need to limit the rise of global temperature to 2°C, 1.5°C if possible, all the while failing to name a single concrete measure that would render that target realistic, or at least likely – thus generating the bitter suspicion that a supposed inevitability of the "Plan B" of geo-engineering is the ghost that animates its machine.[2]

From a point of view that we could call dialogical rather than critical, however, the most important fact to produce a virtual modification of the context of reception of the present book was the publication of Bruno Latour's *Face à Gaïa* (2015). The latter is an extensively and intensively revamped version of *Facing Gaia*, the Gifford Lectures on Natural Religion presented by the author in Edinburgh in 2013, and which have served as a sort of underlying narrative thread for *The Ends of the World*. *Face à Gaïa* was written taking into account, among several other texts, our own "L'Arrêt de Monde." To incorporate Latour's book into ours would effectively entail writing a different book altogether. All we can therefore do is suggest that *The Ends of the World* be read alongside *Face à Gaïa* (forthcoming in English translation as *Facing Gaia*, Polity Press, 2017), so that readers can draw their own conclusions.

In short, if we have chosen to publish *Há Mundo Por Vir?* without taking into due account all these subsequent developments, it is because we strongly believe that the observations contained herein, the positions that are contested as well as defended, do not require any correction or elaboration that would modify this book's analyses or central theses.

Finally, we would like to add a couple of technical notes. Firstly: the symbol § indicates passages that are digressions from the main argument, but are intended to add depth of explanation to the text in the same way that an extended footnote world. Secondly: in the Gifford Lectures, Latour renders the French *Terriens* as "Earthlings" or, more frequently, as "Earthbound people," playing on the adjective's multiple connotations: the people who are *destined to* the Earth, who are *tied to* the Earth, who are *under the spell of* the Earth... We have chosen the name "Terrans" to designate this demos, which, as shall be seen, Latour opposes to "Humans" and/or "Moderns," taken as synonymous ways of referring to the same people, namely, "us". *Who* these "Terrans" are is one of the central problems in our book.

Acknowledgments

The first draft of this text was an oral presentation made on December 21, 2012 (the day of the end of the world according to a supposedly "Mayan" calendar), at the Université de Toulouse-Le Mirail, at the behest of the *Equipe de Recherche sur les Rationalités Philosophiques et les Savoirs* [Philosophical Rationalities and Knowledges Research Team] (ERRAPHIS); and, a few weeks later, in a seminar in the *Expérimentation Arts et Politiques* [Experimentation in Art and Politics] (SPEAP) program at the Institute of Political Studies (Sciences Po) in Paris. We thank Jean-Christophe Goddard and Bruno Latour respectively for the invitations, as well as those who attended the lectures for their welcome and comments. Jean-Christophe, Gwen-Elen, and Jeanne Goddard hosted us in Toulouse with a warmth that was nothing less than moving. Bruno Latour, old friend that he is, deserves special thanks for being not only our greatest motivator but also, as shall become obvious, our main interlocutor.

We would also like to thank our brave fellow Terran people of #ATOA, Alexandre Nodari, Flávia Cera, Marcos de Almeida Matos, and Rondinelly Gomes de Medeiros, who have been with us from the start, and most especially since the "anthropolemical" event *terrAterra*, which took place as part of the People's Summit parallel to the Rio+20 Climate Conference, in 2012; to Idelber Avelar, who first pointed us in the direction of Dipesh Chakrabarty's article, and for his ever generous support to the Terran cause; to Rodrigo Nunes, for several indications regarding speculative realism, accelerationism, and their surroundings; to Felipe Süssekind, Alyne de Castro Costa, Juliana Fausto, Marco Antônio Valentim, Cecilia Cavalieri, José Marcio Fragoso, André Vallias, and Moysés Pinto Neto, for their complicity and decisive support in more than one skirmish in the ongoing war of the worlds. We shall win.

The Ends of the World is an updated, expanded version of the essay "L'Arrêt de monde," translated from Portuguese into French by Oiara Bonilla (whom we thank for her patience) and published in June 2014 in the book *De l'Univers Clos au Monde Infini* (Hache 2014). We are grateful to Émilie Hache, who invited us to contribute to that collection, for her kind decision to publish the text in its entirety and her valuable editorial suggestions (a gratitude we also extend to our friend Élie Kongs). It falls to Michael Houseman, finally, who dedicated a cold afternoon in 2013 to comment on one of the first oral versions of the text and who has, with Marika Moisseeff, hosted us so many times in the course of so many years with unconditional and infinitely graceful friendship, to close a list of acknowledgments that should have extended much farther.

Acknowledgments for quotations in text

p. ix: Lispector, Clarice (1999) *Para Não Esquecer (Crônicas)*. Rio de Janeiro: Rocco.

Chapter 2, p. 1: Thom Yorke. From the song "Idiotheque" by Thomas Edward Yorke (author of lyrics), Philip James Selway, Edward John O'Brien, Colin Charles Greenwood, Jonathan Greenwood, Richard Guy and Paul Lansky, on the album *Kid A* (2000) by Radiohead. Warner/Chappell Music Ltd and Warner/Chappell Music Publishing Ltd.

Chapter 4, p. 1: Don Juan Matus, cited in Carlos Castañeda (1992) *Tales of Power*. New York: Washington Square Press (reissue edition 1992; original 1974).

Chapter 5, p. 1: T. S. Eliot, 'The Hollow Men', in T. S. Eliot (1991) *Collected Poems 1909–1962*. San Diego/New York/

London: Harcourt Brace Jovanovich, Copyright 1936 by Houghton Mifflin Harcourt Publishing Company. Copyright © renewed 1964 by Thomas Stearns Eliot. Reprinted by permission of Houghton Mifflin Harcourt Publishing Company. All rights reserved. Reprinted outside of the US by permission of Faber and Faber Ltd.

p. ix and chapter 7, p. 95: Davi Kopenawa and Bruce Albert, *The Falling Sky: Words of a Yanomami Shaman*. Translated by Nicholas Elliott and Alison Dundy, Cambridge, Mass.: The Belknap Press of Harvard University Press, Copyright © 2013 by the President and Fellows of Harvard College.

Conclusion, p. 1: From 'What is Philosophy?', by Felix Guattari and Gilles Deleuze. Copyright © 1996 Columbia University Press. Reprinted with permission of the publisher.

1

What rough beast...

The end of the world is a seemingly interminable topic – at least, of course, until it happens. The ethnographic record documents a variety of ways in which human cultures have imagined the disarticulation of the spatio-temporal frameworks of history. Some of these imaginings have had a new lease of life since the 1990s, when scientific consensus became established regarding the ongoing changes in the planet's thermodynamic regime. Information on the (anthropic) causes and (catastrophic) consequences of the planetary "crisis" have accumulated at a speedy rate, mobilizing popular perception as well as academic reflection.

As the gravity and irreversibility of the present environmental and civilizational crisis become more and more evident,[1] there has been a growing proliferation of new and old variations on a theme that we shall call, for the sake of a simplicity that this essay intends to complicate somewhat, "the end of the world." There have been blockbusters of the fantasy genre,[2] History Channel docufictions, scientific popularization books of varying complexity, videogames, art and music pieces, blogs of all shades across the ideological spectrum, academic journals and specialized networks, reports and pronouncements issued by world organizations of all kinds, unerringly frustrating global climate conferences (like the COPs), theology symposia and papal pronouncements, philosophical tracts, New Age and neo-pagan ceremonies, an exponentially rising number of political manifestos – in short, texts, contexts, vehicles, speakers, and audiences of all kinds. The presence of this theme in contemporary culture has increased as much and as rapidly as what it refers to – namely, the intensifying changes in the terrestrial macro-environment.

This veritable disphoric efflorescence goes against the grain of the "humanist" optimism that was predominant in the last three or four centuries of Western history. It is a harbinger, if not already a reflection, of something that seemed excluded from the horizon of history qua the saga of Spirit: the ruin of our global civilization as a consequence of its very hegemony. A fall that may drag with it a sizeable portion of human population, obviously beginning with the destitute masses that inhabit the ghettos and garbage dumps of the world system; but the nature of the oncoming catastrophe is such that it will hit us all in one way or another. Therefore, it is not only the dominant, Western, Christian, capitalist civilizational matrix, but the human species as a whole, and the very idea of a human species, that is being interpellated by this crisis. Above all (and for good reason), those peoples, cultures, and societies who are not responsible for said crisis, not to mention several thousand other lineages of living beings who are under threat of extinction or who have already disappeared from the face of the earth thanks to the environmental modifications brought about by "human" actions.[3]

Such a demographic and civilizational disaster is sometimes imagined as the result of a "global" event, a sudden extinction of all human or terrestrial life resulting from either an "act of God" (a lethal supervirus, a massive volcanic explosion, a collision with a celestial body, a giant solar storm), the cumulative effect of anthropic interventions on the Earth System[4] (as in Roland Emmerich's 2004 film *The Day After Tomorrow*), or finally a good old-style nuclear war. On other occasions, the disaster tends to be more realistically depicted, in line with the successive scenarios proposed by the so-called climate sciences, as a *process*. A relentless, extremely intense, already ongoing, increasingly accelerating and in many respects irreversible process, a deterioration of the environmental conditions that presided over human life during the Holocene,[5] in which droughts follow hurricanes and floods, human and animal pandemics follow colossal crop losses, and genocidal wars take place against the background of extinctions that affect whole genera, families, and even phyla. All of which would act back on each other in perverse feedback loops that would slowly but inexorably push our species, in a process of "slow violence" (Nixon 2011) that appears to become less and less slow, toward a materially and politically sordid existence – what Isabelle Stengers (2015) has dubbed "the coming barbarism," and which will be all the more barbaric if the dominant techno-economic system (which we could call, with a nod to Félix Guattari, Integrated World Capitalism) is allowed to continue its headlong flight forward from itself unchecked.

It is not only the natural sciences, and the mass culture feeding off them, which have been registering the world's drift. Even metaphysics, notoriously the most ethereal of philosophical fields, has begun to echo the generalized disquiet. The last years have seen, for example, the elaboration of new and sophisticated conceptual arguments that propose to "end the world" in their own way:[6] be it to end the world conceived as being inescapably a world-for-man, so as to justify full epistemic access to a "world-without-us" which would articulate itself absolutely prior to the legislative intervention of the Understanding; be it to end the world-as-meaning, so as to determine Being as pure indifferent exteriority – as if the "real" world, in its radical contingency and purposelessness, had to be "realized" *against* Reason and Meaning.

It is true that many of these metaphysical ends-of-the-world have only an indirect motivational relationship to the physical event of planetary catastrophe; but that does not make them any less expressive of it, offering as they do an outlet for the vertiginous sensation of incompatibility – perhaps even incompossibility – between the human and the world. Few areas of contemporary imagination have failed to be affected by the violent re-entry of the Western noosphere into the Earth's atmosphere, in a veritable and unique process of "transdescendence." We once believed ourselves destined to a vast sidereal ocean, now we find ourselves thrown back at the harbor whence we started...

Dystopias, then, proliferate; and a certain perplexed panic (pejoratively indicted as "catastrophism"), if not a sort of grim satisfaction (recently popularized under the name of "accelerationism"), seems to hover over the spirit of the times. The predictive value of punk's famous cry of "no future" is revitalized – if that is the right word – at the same time as previous anxieties return, comparable in scope and intensity to our present ones, such as those elicited by the nuclear arms race of the not-so-distant years of the Cold War. It is impossible not to remember Günther Anders' (2007: 112–13) dry, somber conclusion in a capital text on human-kind's "metaphysical metamorphosis" after Hiroshima and Nagasaki: "The absence of future has already begun."

This future-that-is-over is thus come once again, suggest-ing that it maybe never stopped having already begun. (In the Neolithic? In the Industrial Revolution? In the atomic era?) If the prospect of the climate crisis is less spectacular than that of the nuclear threat (which has never gone away, lest we forget), its ontology is more complex, both in what regards its connections to human agency and in its paradoxi-cal chronotopics.[7] Its advent bears the name of the species: "Anthropocene," the designator proposed by Paul Crutzen and Eugene Stoermer for what they see as the new geologi-cal epoch that came after the Holocene, which would have started with the Industrial Revolution and become intensified after World War II.

§ On the somewhat paradoxical relationship between the emer-gence of a "biospheric" consciousness, the perspective from outer space, the consolidation of climate change theory and the Cold War's arms race (Reagan's *Star Wars* program included), the reader will find the works of Joseph Masco (2010, 2012) and Peter Szendy (2011) of interest. In a recent TED talk, James Hansen (2012), speaking of the temporary energetic disequi-librium of the Earth System caused by the build-up of green-house gases (the difference between the amount of energy or heat that enters the system and the amount reflected back into space), suggested an eloquent equivalence between the heat of $0.58 \text{ W}/m^2$ daily accumulated in the planet's "reservoirs" (the oceans, ice caps and soil) and the heat liberated by the explo-sion of four hundred thousand atomic bombs. On that topic, see also John Cook's excellent *Skeptical Science* blog, according to which our climate has accumulated an amount of heat equivalent to the explosion of four Hiroshima bombs per second, totaling 2,115,122,880 bombs from 1998 until the time of writing (to be precise, July 2, 2014, 2.45 p.m. Brazilian time, when we last consulted the <http://4hiroshimas.com> widget).[8] (For an illustration of the strongly symbolic relation – the "prolonged hesitation between sound and sense," as Valéry would say – between the names "Hiroshima" and "Katrina," see AAP 2013.) In short, the old human project of continuously increasing the amount of per capita energy (Lévi-Strauss 1952: 32) at our disposal finally seems, since the acceleration of the processes through which this energy is obtained after the Industrial Revolution, to be coming up against a wall into which the species runs the risk of colliding in a most spectacular way.

Although others had apparently already proposed terms like "Anthroposphere," "Anthrocene," or "Anthropocene" in the last century (and even earlier), it is said that it was during a discussion at a meeting of the International Geosphere-Biosphere Programme (IGBP) in Mexico City in 2000 that the atmospheric chemist and Nobel Prize laureate Paul Crutzen first proposed the concept, publishing an article on the subject shortly afterwards (Crutzen and Stoermer 2000), formalizing it two years later (Crutzen 2002). The proposal is still under consideration by the scientific community, and should be discussed at the next International Congress of Geology in August 2016. Crutzen has recently stated that he is inclined to suggest the twentieth century's nuclear tests as marking the diagnostic beginning ("golden spike") of the Anthropocene.

The Anthropocene, or whatever else one might want to call it,[9] is an "epoch" in the geological sense of the word; but it points toward the end of epochality as such, insofar as our species is concerned. For it is certain that, although it began with us, it will end without us: the Anthropocene will only give way to a new geological epoch long after we have disappeared from the face of the Earth. Our present is the Anthropocene; this is our time. But this present time progressively reveals itself a present "without a view," a *passive* present, the inert bearer of a geophysical karma which it is entirely beyond our reach to cancel, which makes the duty of its mitigation all the more urgent and demanding: "the revolution has already occurred...the events we have to cope with do not lie in the future, but largely in the past

...[W]hatever we do now, the threat will remain with us for centuries, for millennia" (Latour 2013a: 109).

Metaphysics and mythophysics

This essay is an attempt to take present discourses on the end of the world seriously, grasping them as thought experiments about the downward turn of the Western anthropological adventure, that is, as efforts, though not necessarily intentional ones, to invent a mythology that is adequate to our times. The "end of the world" is one of those famous types of problems of which Kant used to say human reason cannot solve, but cannot help posing at the same time either; and it does so necessarily in the form of mythical fabulation or, as it is fashionable to say nowadays, of "narratives" that orient and motivate us. The semiotic regime of myth, perfectly indifferent to the empirical truth or falsity of its contents, comes into play whenever the relation between humans as such and their most general conditions of existence imposes itself as a problem for reason. And if it is true that all mythology could be described as a schematization of certain transcendental conditions in empirical terms – a validating retroprojection of certain sufficient reasons in terms of certain efficient causes – then the present impasse becomes all the more tragic, or ironic, given that such a problem of Reason has now been given the stamp of the Understanding: here is an essentially metaphysical problem, the end of the world, formulated in the rigorous terms of such supremely empirical sciences as climatology, geophysics, and biochemistry. Maybe, as Lévi-Strauss often remarked, science, which started out by separating itself from myth around three thousand years ago, will eventually encounter it once again at the end of one of those "double twists" which tie analytic to dialectical reason, the anagrammatic combinatory of the signifier to the historical vicissitudes of the signified.[10]

One word more on the notion of "myth." An important, if contingent, stimulus to the present essay comes from a book of philosophy, Quentin Meillassoux's *After Finitude* (2009), originally published in French in 2006. Alongside the writings of other contemporary thinkers associated with so-called "speculative realism," Meillassoux's project seemed to us to renew, *nolens volens*, the ties between metaphysical speculation and the mythological (Kant would say "dogmatic") matrix of all thought. After reading *After Finitude* (and later on Ray Brassier's 2007 *Nihil Unbound*, another influential work in the speculative realist movement), our impression was that the book inscribed itself in a series stretching, say, from Saint Anselm to Badiou, but *also* in a vast discursive universe that goes from the treasure trove of ideas accrued over millennia in the cosmological speculation of the world's indigenous peoples up until Lars Von Trier's (2011) *Melancholia* and Cormac McCarthy's (2006) *The Road*, by way of the long Western mythico-literary tradition on the theme of the *pays gaste* or "wasteland" (Weston 1920), and the persistent vitality of this "minor" genre which is science fiction.[11] Jorge Luis Borges' (2007) well-known quip on metaphysics being a branch of fantastic literature not only requires that the converse be true – fantastic literature and science fiction are the pop metaphysics (or the "mythophysics") of our time – but it effectively anticipated the cross-pollination currently taking place between some experiments in the creative fringe of contemporary philosophy and the work of "popular" writers like H. P. Lovecraft, Philip K. Dick, Ursula Le Guin, William Gibson, David Brin, or China Miéville.

Our goal is then to draw a preliminary balance sheet of some of the main variants of the "end of the world" theme, such as it presents itself today in the imaginary of world culture. But let us begin by briefly evoking the problem's so-called objective terms.

2

...Its hour come round
at last...

We're not scaremongering
This is really happening
Thom Yorke

Gaia and anthropos

Recalling the ancient Chinese curse, we can say we live in interesting times. One of the most interesting aspects of our time, as has been observed time and again, is its acceleration; time is out of joint, and it is running faster. "Things are changing so fast that it is hard to keep track," Bruno Latour (2013a: 126) remarked recently. He was referring to the state of scientific knowledge regarding the problem;[1] but for some time now it has been time itself, as the dimension of the manifestation of change (time as "the number of motion," as per Aristotle), that seems to be not only speeding up, but qualitatively changing *all the time*. Virtually everything that can be said about the climate crisis becomes, *ipso facto*, anachronistic, out of step; and everything that can be done about it is necessarily too little, too late. This metatemporal instability is conjoined with a sudden insufficiency of world – let us recall the argument about the five Earths it would take to extend the average US citizen's energy consumption level to humankind at large – which is producing in us something like an experience of the decomposition of time (the end) and space (the world), and the surprising downgrade of these two a priori conditions of sensibility to the status of forms *conditioned* by human action.[2] This is one of the ways, and not the least important, in which it can be said that our world has ceased to be Kantian. Intriguingly enough, everything takes place as if, of the three great transcendental ideas identified by Kant – God, Soul, and World, respectively the objects of theology, psychology, and cosmology – we were now watching the downfall of the last. After God died somewhere between the eighteenth and nineteenth centuries and the Soul at some later point (its semi-empirical avatar, Man, having perhaps survived until the mid-twentieth century), the World had soldiered on as the last, wavering rampart of metaphysics (Gaston 2013: ix).

Human history has known several crises, but the so-called "global civilization," the arrogant name we give to the worldwide expansion of capitalist economy based on fossil-fuel technologies, has never faced a global threat such as the ongoing one. We are not just talking about global warming and climate change. In September 2009, *Nature* published a special issue in which several scientists, coordinated by Johan Rockström of the Stockholm Resilience Centre, identified nine biophysical processes of the Earth System and sought to establish limits to these processes which, if crossed, would lead to environmental alterations that would be unbearable to several species, ours included: climate change, ocean acidification, stratospheric ozone depletion, global freshwater use, biodiversity loss, interference with the nitrogen and phosphorus cycles, changes in land use, chemical pollution, and atmospheric aerosol loading. By way of conclusion, the authors warned that "[w]e do not have the luxury of concentrating our efforts on any one of them in isolation from the others. If one boundary is transgressed, then other boundaries are also under serious risk" (Rockström et al. 2009: 474). Except that, according to them, it may just be that we have already left the safety zone for three of these processes – biodiversity loss, human interference with the nitrogen cycle (the rate at which N2 is removed from the atmosphere and converted into reactive nitrogen for human use), and climate change – and we are very close to the limit of the other three – fresh water use, change in land use, and ocean acidification.[3]

One of the canaries in the coalmine of climate change is the melting of the Earth's main ice caps. The fourth report by the Intergovernmental Panel on Climate Change (IPCC), issued in 2007, estimated that Arctic sea ice could disappear by the end of the century. Yet the region's ice-melt record was broken in August 2012, and some scientists hazarded the prediction of an iceless summer in the Arctic in this decade. In 2013's fifth report, the executive summary of the findings of the IPCC's Working Group 1 classified as "probable" the total absence of sea ice in the Arctic in the months of September by the *middle* of the century. But the latest news items from the polar regions are yet posterior to the IPCC fifth report, and refer to the frightening speed at which monumental glaciers are melting in Greenland and the Antarctic, which modifies the spatial and temporal predictions regarding sea-level rise stated in that text. Paraphrasing the *Communist Manifesto*, all that is solid – beginning with the Earth's oldest ice – melts into the sea.[4]

§ Ocean acidification has often been talked about as climate change's twin sister, as it shares the same causes and has equally grave consequences for the future of life on the planet. It is important to stress that the "planetary boundaries" were tentatively proposed; there was no absolute certainty, on the part of the very scientists who took part in the Stockholm Resilience Centre study, regarding the quantification of some of the parameters in question. For the sake of getting a sense of the discussion pertinent to the first version of the study, we refer the reader, for example, to Barnosky et al. (2012), which reinforces the idea of a global tipping point for the Earth's biosphere, and Brook et al. (2013), which questions the existence of such a tipping point specifically in relation to the loss of biodiversity. For a serious and stimulating attempt at a critical but optimistic – since the authors seem to believe in the possibility of a "good Anthropocene" – rendering of the theme of planetary boundaries from a broadly anthropological viewpoint, see Pálsson et al. (2013), who insist that a theoretical and practical confrontation with environmental catastrophe calls for an urgent reconsideration of the expertise of what English speakers call, with that hesitant connective, "the social sciences *and* humanities." "Nature" or "the environment," in short, would be something too serious to be left to the hands (and research budgets, needless to say) of natural scientists only; all the more so when the distinction between "ambient" and "ambiented," nature and culture, becomes increasingly problematic both theoretically and empirically. It is difficult to disagree with the authors' plea and the reasoning that led them to it, in particular the argument according to which, while the "natural" sciences of the Earth System are capable of parameterizing and modeling the geophysical evolution of the planetary crisis, the contribution of the humanities is nonetheless indispensable if we are to comprehend its sociopolitical consequences, articulate possible responses to it, and establish acceptable compromises for a "humankind" that presents itself *immediately* as split into collectives with variable and conflicting interests and understandings of what they deem as the most important life values, and whose future condition, the authors emphasize, will probably be as different from today's Integrated World Capitalism as from the medieval world or Paleolithic societies. (That is not necessarily an optimistic prediction, it should be clear.) What we are less enthusiastic about, however, is the critical cliché that functions as a leitmotiv in Pálsson et al.'s (2013: 8) text: the idea that "it is important to historicize and contextualize claims about limits and boundaries." Of course it is, and it is indeed imperative; provided, however, that such admonition does not lead us to the dispiriting conclusion that "limits and boundaries" are just another "social construction." A similar observation is equally adequate to other fundamentally sound caveats that are found in the same article, such as:

> There is a need to pay more attention to the social distribution of the planetary impacts, which are not always easily quantifiable. The imbalance in fresh-water availability, for instance, can hardly be resolved by global redistribution, which poses particular governance problems. 'A safe operating space for humanity' might be a useful tool on the global scale, but is a fiction on smaller scales. (Ibid.: 7)

§ "Governance," "resources," "environmental services"... Apart from the managerial language that surfaces here and there in the text – associated with the idea of "sustainability," of which we would say that it might be a useful tool on the local scale, but is a fiction on larger ones – we cannot but draw attention to how naturally the dichotomy between "local" and "global" is maintained, when that is precisely one of the aspects that are objectively most challenged by the planetary crisis.[5] It would be a shame if we once again ended up reconstituting the Nature/ Culture dualism through the very same gestures that denounce it as null and void, opposing natural scientists mesmerized by "geophysical parameters" and equipped with a vague notion of "humankind" endowed with little political efficacy, whilst social scientists simply rename as "environmental justice" the perennial, uncircumventable struggle of the wretched of the Earth for rights – what used to be called "social justice." As one of the founding slogans of Brazil's Instituto Socioambiental[6] (Socio-Environmental Institute) stated back in the 1990s, "socio-environmental is a single word." To put it differently, we find it necessary to understand the notion of *political ecology* as a pleonasm with a strictly emphatic sense, not as a hybrid conceptual compromise between a Nature and a Culture whose separation would ultimately, if only in an underhand way, still go unchallenged. But maybe we are reading the call to arms issued by the authors of that article in less than charitable terms – for which we apologize as the case may be.

In short, we are about to enter – or have already entered, the uncertainty itself being an evidence of runaway temporality – a regime of the Earth System that is quite unlike anything we have ever known. The *near* future becomes unpredictable, if not indeed unimaginable outside the framework of science-fiction scenarios or messianic eschatologies.

There are several impressive icons of the acceleration of environmental changes at a rate that has become perceptible in the span of one or two human generations, such as the "hockey stick"[7] graphs showing the vertiginous rise in certain critical parameters (average global temperatures, population growth, per capita energy consumption, species extinction rate, etc.) from the end of the nineteenth century on, or the Keeling curve, describing the evolution in the rate of CO_2 concentration in the atmosphere since 1960, which hit the 400 ppm milestone on May 9, 2014.[8] It is therefore not just a matter of the magnitude of change in relation to some benchmark (for instance, 280 ppm of CO_2 concentration before the Industrial Revolution), but of its *increasing acceleration* – the intensification of variation, and the consequent loss of any benchmark. Each year seems to establish a "new normal" for climate parameters – which is to say that abnormality has become the norm.

We live in a time of catastrophic points and curve reversals.[9] Record-breaking high temperatures are followed more and more often by record-breaking low temperatures in unexpected places, even if the global trend points up. There are almost daily debates on the speeding rate of CO_2 concentration, which involves, among other things, a discussion on the economy of developing countries; there are debates about the "sensitivity" of the Earth System and the resulting rate of rise in global temperature in relation to the doubling of the amount of CO_2 accumulated in the system. On the other hand, the global decrease in the volume of ice does not prevent a (provisional?) increase in the area thereof in some parts of the planet (the Antarctic), which goes together with its change in consistency, color, and therefore also its albedo or capacity to reflect sunlight. What are the expected rate and proportion of sea-level rise, for instance, and what is the cause of the mysterious drop in the general global sea-level rise that occurred between 2010 and 2011?[10] How are we to account for the problem of climate change attribution, and how to speak of deviation from the norm if the norm itself is changing with every new year?[11] Hotter and colder, drier and wetter, faster and slower, clearer and darker; now more, now less sensitivity or reflectivity. The instability affects time, quantities, qualities, measures and scales themselves; it also corrodes space. Local and global are superposed and blur into each other: sea rise is not globally uniform; climate change is a global phenomenon, but extreme climate events strike now here, now there, making their prediction and the prevention of their impacts ever more difficult. Everything we do locally has consequences for the global climate, yet our little individual actions of mitigation seem to have no observable effect whatsoever. We are trapped, that is, in a generalized becoming-mad of the extensive and intensive quantities that express the Earth's biogeophysical system. One should therefore not be surprised that some climatologists already refer to the present climate system as "the climate beast."[12]

What all of this suggests is that the acceleration of time – and the correlative compression of space – usually seen as an existential or psychocultural condition of Western modernity, has just crossed over from sociocultural into biogeophysical history in an objectively paradoxical way. It is this passage that Dipesh Chakrabarty (2009) describes in his trailblazing article "The Climate of History: Four Theses" as the transformation of our species from a mere biological *agent* into a geological *force*. This is the most significant phenomenon of the present century: "the intrusion of Gaia" (Stengers 2015), brusque and abrupt, into the horizon of human history; the sensation of a definitive return of a form of transcendence that we believed transcended, and which reappears in more formidable form than ever. The transformation of humans into a geological force, that is, into an "objective" phenomenon or "natural" object, is paid back with the intrusion of Gaia in the human world, giving the Earth System the menacing form of a historical subject, a political agent, a moral person (Latour 2013a). In an ironic and deadly (because recursively contradictory) inversion of the relation between figure and ground, the *ambiented* becomes the *ambient* (or "ambienting"), and the converse is equally the case. It is effectively the collapse of an ever more ambiguous environment, of which we can no longer say *where* it is in relation to us, and us to it.[13]

This sudden collision of Humans with the Earth, the terrifying (or terrafying) communication of the geopolitical and the geophysical, contributes decisively to the crumbling of the foundational distinction of the modern *episteme* – the one between the cosmological and anthropological orders, separated since "forever" (namely, at least since the seventeenth century) by a double discontinuity, in essence and in scale. The evolution of the species on one side, the history of capitalism on the other (in the long run, we are all dead); everything is thermodynamics at bottom, but the dynamic of the stock market is the matter that really matters; quantum events fluctuate at the heart of reality, but it is the uncertainties of parliamentary politics that really mobilize our hearts and minds...In other (and fewer) words, it is the split between Nature and Culture that we are talking about (Latour 1993; Viveiros de Castro 2012a). And yet here we are: once the protective dome that both separated us from and infinitely elevated us above the infinite Nature "out there" is broken (Hache and Latour 2010), we find ourselves in the Anthropocene, the age when geology has come into a properly *geological* resonance with morality, as those celebrated visionaries Deleuze and Guattari (1987) had predicted a full twenty years before Crutzen. (Which, it must be said, does not so much moralize geology – human responsibility, intentionality, meaning; see Pálsson et al. 2013 – but properly speaking geologizes morals.)[14] The beautiful sociocosmological stratification of modernity starts to implode before our very eyes; it was thought that the edifice could stand on its ground floor alone (the economy), but it turns out we had forgotten the foundations; and panic arises when it transpires that determination in the last instance may not actually have the final word...

Not only was modernity globalized but the planetary globe was modernized, all in a very short interval of time: "it is only very recently that the distinction between human and natural histories...has begun to collapse" (Chakrabarty 2009: 207). The idea that our species is a newcomer on the planet, that history as we know it (agriculture, cities, writing) is even more recent, and that the energy-intensive, fossil-fuel based industrial way of life began only a second ago in terms of *Homo sapiens'* evolutionary clock all seem to point to the conclusion that humankind itself is a catastrophe: a sudden, devastating event in the planet's biological and geophysical history, one that will disappear much faster than the changes it will have occasioned in the Earth's thermodynamic regime and biological balance. In the accounts bequeathed to us by this "deep history" being told by historians, paleontologists, climatologists, and geologists, humans play a role that is at once crucial, belated, and very probably ephemeral.[15]

§ On the likely scientific mistake and doubtlessly convenient political maneuver of dating the beginning of the Anthropocene back to the Neolithic, thus exculpating the present techno-economic interests that fill the atmosphere with CO_2 (or at least attenuating the gravity of their crimes), we refer the reader to Hamilton (2014). Apart from contesting that retreat, Hamilton reminds us that there are widely regarded paleoclimatologists, such as Wally Broecker, who would rather speak of a new geological *era* (the "Anthropozoic") than of an *epoch* (the Anthropocene), thus increasing in at least one order of magnitude the chronological scale and the geophysical significance of the event that began with the Industrial Revolution and its successive stages of intensification.[16] Let us also bear in mind that the idea of a congenital ecocidal condition of *Homo sapiens* is frequently evoked – with the best of intentions at times[17] – in order to explain the present anthropocenic debacle. However, that argument has been met with skepticism by at least some paleo-ecologists close to "resilience theory" (Brooke 2014: 8–9; 267–8), who suggest, on the contrary, that there were exceedingly long periods of ecological and sociopolitical stability in archaic societies, punctuated by exogenous environmental bottlenecks (non-Malthusian catastrophes of tectonic or astronomical origin). In a line of argument similar to Monbiot's on *Homo destructor*, Pálsson et al. (2013: 8) suggest that what is "most striking" about the Anthropocene is that it is the first geological epoch in which a macrophysically determinant force is "actively conscious of its geological role," and that this potentially modifies the very nature of geology. Yet would that not be more or less equivalent to saying that, after Darwin, the laws of evolution have been "potentially" modified, that is, that we now are capable of infringing them? It is a curious argument. Is being *actively* conscious of one's geological role necessarily synonymous with being actively *capable* of changing that behavior? After all, we have been "actively conscious" of our mortality for hundreds of millennia perhaps, and still...

We shall see further on that the term "Anthropocene," or at least its geophysical-anthropological reference, does not inspire unanimous enthusiasm among specialists in the "humanities." For the time being, let us just evoke here the proposal – very characteristic, all in all, of one of the main strains of critique surrounding the concept – to rename it as the "Capitalocene." Its greatest champion is sociologist Jason Moore, coordinator of the World Ecology Research Network.[18] As Moore sees it, the Industrial Revolution begun in the nineteenth century is only the consequence of a socio-economic mutation that spawned capitalism in the "long sixteenth century," and the crisis therefore ultimately stems from changes in the relations of production rather than (and before) the productive forces, if we can put it that way. (That would entail, one presumes, that it was after all not the windmill that gave us the feudal lord, nor the steam engine the industrial capitalist.) However, as Chakrabarty has pointed out:

> Some scholars argue that it is not human agency as such that has become a planetary force, climate change is simply a result of capitalist development. "It is capitalism, stupid!" is their refrain. If you pointed out to them that a Soviet-type modernization of the world would have produced very similar consequences, some of them would engage in

a lot of theoretic jiu-jitsu to prove that Soviet socialism was actually capitalism in another form! (Of course, one can't argue about a "true socialism" that nobody has seen. (Chakrabarty 2012)[19]

Naturally, the empirical finitude of our species is something that the vast majority of Western-educated people have learned to admit since, say, at least Darwin. We know that "the world and life started without us and will end without us," as in Lévi-Strauss' (1961: 397) oft-remembered, and oft-plagiarized, statement. But when the scales of collective and individual finitude enter into a convergent trajectory, this cognitive truth suddenly becomes an inconvenient *affective* truth to manage. It is one thing to know that the Earth and even the entire universe will disappear come billions of years, or that, long before that but in a still indeterminate future, the human species will become extinct – even though the latter knowledge is often sublimated by the hope that we will morph into "another species," even if that notion is lacking in any precise meaning. It is another, rather different thing to imagine the situation posited by present scientific knowledge within our field of imminent possibilities: that the next generations (the generations next *to us*) will have to survive in an impoverished, sordid environment; an ecological desert, a sociological hell. In other words, it is one thing to theoretically know that we will die; it is another to receive news from our doctor, test results in hand, that we are suffering from a terminal disease.

§ One thing that heightens the difficulty of thinking the catastrophe is the "hyperobjective" character of climate change. "Hyperobject" is the name given by Timothy Morton (2010, 2013) to a relatively new type of phenomena and/or entities that, according to him, defy our perception of time and space because, among other things, they persist and produce effects whose duration enormously exceeds the individual and collective scales of human life, not to mention (quite plausibly) the duration of the species. Examples of hyperobjects are radioactive materials and other kinds of industrial waste, as well as global warming and the transformations that will follow from it, which can last for thousands or millions of years until the conditions known today are re-established. Authors such as Hans Jonas and Günther Anders, it should be noted, had by and large already anticipated this idea of a radical disproportion, occasioned by the demiurgic powers of modern technology, between causes and effects, actions and consequences, in a process of delocalization and eternization of human actions – from the point of view, that is, of our experience and imagination.[20]

As Latour (2013a: 109; our emphasis) points out, trying to bring out the various aspects of the feeling of "disconnection" that paralyzes us in the face of present events: "*Nothing [is] at the right scale.*" We are therefore not only dealing with a "crisis" *in* time and space, but a ferocious corrosion *of* time and space.[21] This phenomenon of a generalized collapse of spatial and temporal scales (the contemporary interest in fractals being in no way accidental) heralds the rise of a critical continuity between the rhythms of nature and culture, a sign that indicates a massive, imminent phase transition in human historical experience. We are thus forced to recognize (once again Lévi-Strauss' double twist) the advent of another continuity, a quasi-Freudian *Nachträglichkeit*, or rather a continuity *to-come* between the modern present and the non-modern past – a mythological or, in other words, cosmopolitical continuity. Historical time starts to resonate again with meteorological or "ecological" (Evans-Pritchard 1939) time, though no longer in the archaic terms of seasonal cycles, but in the sense of the disruption of cycles and the irruption of cataclysms. Psychological space becomes coextensive with ecological space, though no longer in the form of magical control over the environment, but as the "*cold panic*" (Stengers 2015: 32; italics in the original) provoked by the enormous rift between scientific knowledge and political impotence – between our (scientific) capacity to imagine the end of the world and our (political) incapacity to imagine the end of capitalism, to repeat yet again Jameson's oft-cited witticism. Apparently, then, we find ourselves not only on the verge of a return to a "pre-modern condition," but we will find ourselves, in the face of our frontal collision with Gaia, even *more* defenseless than so-called "primitive man" found itself before the power of Nature. For the latter at least found itself "protected, and to a certain degree emancipated, by the protective cushion of his dreams" (Lévi-Strauss 1961: 390). Our nightmares assail us while we are wide awake – though

the sensation of being awake might just be one more nightmare among others.

The end-of-the-world perspective

It is this shock that the aforementioned apocalyptic discourses
allude to, whose varied, sometimes discordant effects on the
contemporary imaginary we aim to analyze in these pages.

The end of the world, then. Let us start from the *"end."*
The formula places us in a paradoxical situation, comparable
to the deformation of spatiotemporal parameters discussed
above. In a double movement, it drags us in two opposing
directions, toward a past and a future that are equally double,
each with an "empirical" and a "transcendental" face: the
obscure and violent past of generation (cosmogenesis, anthro-
pogenesis) and the painful future of decadence and corrup-
tion, or of the expectation of death; but also a past of pure
existential plenitude (which was never present as present, as
it is the present's regulative idea and therefore its mythical
inversion) and a future of absolute inexistence (which has
so to speak already happened, since absolute nothingness is
transcendentally retroactive).[22] Every thought of the end of
the world thus poses the question of the beginning of the
world and that of the time before the beginning, the question
of *katechon* (the time of the end, that is, the time-before-the-
end) and that of *eschaton* (the end of times, the ontological
disappearance of time, the end of the end).

Next up comes *"the world."* Thinking the end of the
"world" places us in a register that is at once subtractive
and duplicative: the world is posited in order to be eliminated, posited as *already* eliminated by a thought that is itself
implicated in this elimination, given that it is an (essential or
accidental) aspect, property or dimension of the world, which
at the same time pre-empts the world by representing – or
rather "pre-presenting" – the event of the end. The thought of
the end of the world necessarily evokes the correlate problem
of the end of thought, that is, the end of the (internal or
external) relation between thought and world.

For the sake of argument (that is, without assuming
any ontological commitments), we adopt here the trivial

"correlationist" position that the end of the world is a problem posed by thought, since only thought problematizes – which does not mean (something that is perhaps less trivial) that only humans (or philosophers) "think," that is, have a world to lose. Let us note, in fact, that all the concepts of "world" at play in apocalyptic discourses mobilize a conceptual correlate of the same family as Deleuze's (1990: 301–20) "Other" [*Autrui*]: the Other as a priori structure that is a condition of every possible "objective" world, and thus also of the objective possibility of its extinction.[23] "End of the world" only has a determinate meaning in these discourses – it can only be thought of as possible – on the condition that one determines at the same time *for whom* this world that ends is a *world*, who is the worldly or "worlded" being who *defines the end*. The world, in short, is an *objective perspective*.[24]

The central relation (or correlation) in all these mythical variations on the end of the world – a relation whose end ultimately seems to be what is at issue, even when "the issue" is decentering it or simply de-realizing it – is the relation between "worldliness" and "humankind." In the following pages, the end of the *world* will be examined as something that is necessarily thought from another pole, a *"we"* that includes the (syntactic or pragmatic) subject of the discourse on the end. We shall call "humankind" or "we" this entity for whom the world is a world, or rather, *whose* world the world is.[25] Crucially, however, and this is a point not often remarked by discourses rooted in the perspective of the modern West – whether they are of a "naturalist," "humanist," or "posthumanist" bent – the question of knowing *who* "*we*" *is*, what is understood as "human" or as "person" by *other* collectives consensually regarded (by "us") as humans, is seldom posed, and at any rate never goes beyond the limits of the species as an extensive taxonomic category. Approaching this question is a strategic task, for which empirical anthropology or ethnographic theory is much better prepared than metaphysics or philosophical anthropology, which always seem to know perfectly well what kind of entity the *anthropos* is, and above all who is doing the talking when *one* says "we."[26]

The problem of the end of the world is therefore always formulated as a split or divergence resulting from the disappearance of one of the poles of the duality between the

World and its Inhabitant, that is, the being whose world it is – which, in our metaphysical tradition, normally tends to be the "Human," regardless of whether it goes by the name of *Homo sapiens* or *Dasein*. This disappearance may be due to one term's physical extinction or its metaphysical absorption by its correlative, which in turn necessitates the latter's re-determination. To put it at its simplest, we could start from the opposition between a "world without us," that is, the world after the existence of the human species; and an "us without the world," a worldless or environmentless humankind, the subsistence of some form of humanity or subjectivity after the end of the world. Yet, as we have seen, to think the future disjunction between the terms irresistibly evokes the origin of their present, and precarious, conjunction. The end of the world retroprojects a beginning of the world and, by the same token, humankind's future fate carries us back to its inception. The existence of a "world before us," although it is considered by some to be a philosophical challenge, does not seem too difficult to imagine. But the possibility of an "us before the world," the ontocosmological pre-existence of the human *vis-à-vis* the world, is a much less usual figure in the West's mythological vulgate. We shall see that it is a possibility that has been much explored in Amerindian thought.

The mythical humankind/world duality, thought from the point of view of its dissolution by subtraction of one of the two poles, thus presents us with four basic cases depending on whether we project it into the future or the past. However, this simple fourfold matrix soon unfolds into eight cases, if we consider the affective tone or the value that is attributed to each one of these subtractive resolutions. The world before us can be seen as a Golden Age for life or as a silent, dead desert; humankind after the end of the world can be seen as a race of starbound supermen or a fistful of destitute survivors on a devastated planet; and so forth.[27]

Yet the picture is rather more nuanced, by the sheer fact that the sense and reference of "world" and "people" tend to vary in these artistic, scientific, philosophical, and mythical fabulations. The "subject" or "people" pole seems almost always to refer, as we have seen, to the totality of humankind qua species. But it can also be reduced to the "true" humankind, that is, some specific sociocultural incarnation of human excellence (like us, for example); or, on the contrary, stretch across a universal anthropomorphic virtuality, a sort of background humanity as *prima materia*. As for the "world" whose end is imagined, it might refer to the totality of the terrestrian biosphere; to the cosmos as a "whole" (the ensemble of spatiotemporal entities and processes, that is, the "world" of physics); to Reality in its metaphysical sense, or even Being as such; but it might also denote human socionatural *Umwelt* or, more narrowly, some way of life seen as the only one worthy of true human beings (can we live without planes and computers, plastics and antibiotics?).[28]

These fluctuations or equivocations do not detract from the salience and potency of the idea of "end of the world." Rather, they diffract and multiply them in a variety of ends and of worlds which nonetheless all seem to express the same fundamental historical intuition: it has been disclosed to us that things are changing fast and not for the good of human life "as we know it."[29] Finally, and most crucially, we have no idea what to do about it. The Anthropocene is the Apocalypse, in both the etymological and eschatological senses. Interesting times indeed.

3

...Slouches toward Bethlehem to be born?

The world before us

The mode that we have chosen to start our survey with has its canonical expression in the idea of Eden, a properly paradisiacal image of the world's infancy: the world as it existed until the sixth day of creation, as a stage set for the arrival of the main actor, "Man." Eden is a world-without-humans that is a world-for-humans; humans are the last to come and, in a sense, the world's "end," its finality. Alternatively, we can imagine this world in the week following creation, but before original sin, that is, before Adam and Eve separated themselves from it, objectifying it as their antagonist. The pre-lapsarian world is the pre-objective world of a pre-subjective humankind.[1]

The mythic theme ("mytheme," in structuralist parlance) of the Edenic world persists nowadays in the idea of *wilderness*, those ever more restricted spaces of a pure nature not corrupted by human presence, *horti conclusi* (enclosed gardens) that bear witness to a past that is supposed to have managed to survive "untouched" from the dawn of time until now – but which would today be under threat of disappearing as a result of Western civilization's blindly predatory action. As William Cronon (1995) has rightly shown, it was only at the end of the eighteenth century – partly under the influence of notions such as the "sublime" and the theme of the "last frontier" on the North American imaginary – that wilderness began to be associated with positive affects, with sentiments akin to the sacred, aroused by the contemplation of a magnificent nature conceived as anterior and superior to the human. Before then, the term "wilderness" referred to deserted, desolate, barren, or wild landscapes, which inspired despair, confusion, and the fear of falling under the power of the demonic rather than aesthetic admiration or religiosity. In Milton's *Paradise Lost* (2008: IV, 132–5), the wilderness is the landscape that encloses and protects the Garden of Eden from all outside access. It is this ecotopic obverse of paradise, this anti-Edenic exteriority that Adam and Eve had to face when they were expelled from the cradle, and it was only at the cost of much toil and trouble that they progressively managed to tame and humanize it.

The positive conception of the wilderness as "world without us" is central to many contemporary environmental movements, such as radical preservationism, which enjoyed its most expressive moment in the second half of the twentieth century. This strain of environmentalism considers the existence of human beings as an essentially *denaturing* force, which is why it does not flinch from advocating the expulsion from "natural" spaces of any human collective that might inhabit them (usually indigenous or so-called "traditional" populations, that is, those with little insertion in the capitalist market).[2] Such a post-lapsarian perception of each and every human community is in contrast, or rather confused cohabitation, with an Adamic perception of indigenous populations, according to which these live "in harmony with nature" – which is to say that they have little "impact" on the biophysical parameters of an environment *defined* by the subtraction of the human. Inversely, any transformation of these societies that involves the introduction of industrial objects or techniques into their ways of life suffices to justify their exclusion from this privileged Adamic position – and this then serves, among other things, as an argument to have them expelled from the "wild" lands that they hold on to with all their strength, which invariably turns out in favor of powerful interests with anything but "preservation" at heart. One need only remember how often, in countries like Brazil, the phantom of the "Indian in jeans" (who is therefore "no longer an Indian," and thus "does not need land, just support from social services") is conjured by agribusiness and big landowners with the ever enthusiastic support of corporate media, at once a business partner and servile client of capital.

The Edenic world of wilderness is thus seen as a *plural, organic* world. It is built around a fundamental opposition between *life*, as inexhaustible profusion of forms and subtle balance of forces, and *humankind* (be it as an essentially "anti-natural" species, be it in its modern-industrial variety), imagined as a factor that quantitatively and qualitatively defiles, diminishes, and unbalances life.[3]

The world after us

A second way of framing the opposition between life and humankind consists in projecting it into the future: life will return, invincible in its variety and abundance, reconquering the territory (the Earth) that humankind, acting like an alien, ruthless invader, had transformed into a desert of concrete, tarmac, plastic, and nuclear waste. This paradoxically optimistic take on humankind's disappearance – optimistic given that the adopted point of view is quite clearly that of life itself – is featured in journalist, writer, and environmentalist Alan Weisman's (2007) *The World Without Us*, which has spawned more than one documentary film and TV series.[4] Weisman's book can be seen as a more extreme version of George Stewart's (1949) great sci-fi classic *Earth Abides*, in which one of the few survivors of an epidemic caused by a lethal virus, a naturalist by trade, decides to observe how non-human life evolves after the demise of humans.[5] *The World Without Us*, on the contrary, is a speculative non-fiction describing the planet's fate after our species' absolute end (the cause of which the book does not specify), showing how our material traces will fade away little by little, vanishing for good in a comparatively short time ranging from a couple of decades to a few millennia. After a transitional phase in which "nature" will still have to absorb the explosion of many technological time-bombs left behind by humankind, the end of *Homo sapiens*, along with the ruins of its once

proud civilization, will enable the Earth's flourishing once
again into a vast wilderness, a rich tapestry of ecosystems in
which numberless species thrive. Weisman takes into account
the irreversibility of some anthropic impacts (like climate
change) on the environment that are already in place;[6] but his
thought experiment focuses on nature's capacity to obliter-
ate the material carapace of civilization, revitalizing a planet
suffocated by the accumulation of our artifacts and waste.

§ The same idea of a subtraction of the human allowing for the
planet's Edenic reestablishment is at the heart of the Voluntary
Human Extinction Movement.[7] Created in the early 1990s by US
activist Les Knight, partially inspired by Deep Ecology, the movement preaches our gradual disappearance by means of abstention
from reproduction. The last, already rare humans will be lucky
enough to enjoy this new Eden.

Dipesh Chakrabarty opens "The Climate of History" with
a nod to *The World Without Us*, observing that Weisman's
thought experiment shows how our very sense of history is
threatened with destruction, as a result of the breaking of
the continuity between past and future that gives sense to
our experience of the present. Ecological crisis, taken as the
herald of humankind's empirical finitude, locks historical perspective into a pragmatic paradox: "To go along with Weisman's experiment, we have to insert ourselves into a future
'without us' in order to be able to visualize it" (Chakrabarty
2009: 197–8). The future ceases to be made of the same
matter as the past; it becomes radically *other*, not-ours, a time
that demands our disappearance in order to appear. History
is metaphysically degraded, becoming as transitory as any
historical phenomenon: it is history itself that will soon "be
history." Anders (2007: 11–18), writing a few decades ago,
observed that the fall of geocentric cosmology found itself
rapidly compensated in modern thought with an anthropocentric absolutization of history, that is, by "historical
relativism"; but, he continues, the perspective of the end of
the world opened by the atomic age was an absolute relativ-
ization of this absolutization: the "end of History" becomes
a meteorological occurrence, an accident with a set day and
time to take place, at least *de jure*.

History-that-no-longer-is will be a kind of non-Being fundamentally different to all individual historical events which,
once having passed, cease to be. It will no longer be "past":
it will be something that will have been (or rather, will have
not been) under the form of a never-having-been. (Anders
2007: 22)

In short: we will have never been, period.

The apparent optimism with which Weisman faces his
"world without us" thus proves profoundly ironic, as it
introduces, in the paradoxical mode of its subtraction, a
new global historical actor – humanity as "human species"
or "mankind," a biological entity become geophysical force
capable of destabilizing the boundary parameters of its own
existence.

4

The outside without thought, or the death of the Other

Inside, outside, it really doesn't matter
Don Juan Matus

A certain worldless people of the recent past

It has long been said that modernity's cultural apperception has (or rather had) as one of its fundamental elements a sentiment of worldlessness from which a spiritual crisis of (Western) humankind arose – and whose outcome was the attainment, by that same humankind, of the novel condition of autonomous Subject ("humanity"). The scientific revolution of the seventeenth century, which allegedly freed us from the hierarchical "closed world" and brought us to a democratic "infinite universe" (Koyré 2003) found itself at once rationalized and reversed by the palace coup that was critical philosophy. Kant's misnamed "Copernican Revolution" is, as we know, the source of the official modern conception of Man (let us keep it masculine) as constituent power, the autonomic and sovereign lawgiver of nature, the only being capable of rising above the phenomenal order or causality of which his own understanding is a condition; "human exceptionalism" is a veritable *ontological state of exception*, grounded on the self-grounding separation between Nature and History. The business end of this mythical dispositif was the Promethean image of Man as the conqueror of nature, the being which, emerging from his original animal abjection, lost his world only so as better to regain it as master. But this is a profoundly ambivalent privilege, as we have known since Romanticism at least. The rational appropriation and instrumental economicization of the world led to its "disenchantment" (Weber), and *Dasein*, that "world-former" (Heidegger), reveals himself in the end as a victim of his own success, discovering himself absolutely alone in his "clearing" – the *Lichtung* in the middle of the forest that gives him the monopoly over Being, truth and death. For all its openness, the Clearing cannot but project an inverted image of its external double, the vast, ferocious wilderness surrounding the Garden of Eden.

Modern anthropocentrism or humanism, therefore, corresponds to the "us before the world" scheme, a position of transcendental anteriority of the human which is all the more constitutive of this world the more humans, as empirical beings, show themselves to be constituted by it.[1] And while this anteriority can be seen, on the one hand, as a prerogative – manifest in the creative negativity expressed in every project of "transforming the world" – it can also be denounced and lamented as a degenerate disease: the end of beautiful pagan immanence, the phantasmatic doubling of reality, the betrayal of the Earth, the forgetfulness of Being, a feeling of meaninglessness, relativism, nihilism. Especially in its post-Romantic phase, first with the various existentialisms and, later, with post-modern constructionisms, the rift between subject and world becomes, as Latour has argued in some essential pages, an absolute ontological incommensurability that expresses itself in two complementary mythical figures: that of the world's disappearance, absorbed by the Subject and transformed into his Object (a social construction, a projection of language, a phantasm of desire); but also that of the Subject's disappearance, absorbed by the world and made into a thing among things, an organic contraption assembled by a blind watchmaker. The crisis of what would come to be known as "correlationism" effectively began long before the name was coined.[2]

We do not think it is an exaggeration to say that the Anthropocene, in placing us in the perspective of an "end

of the world" in the most empirical sense possible – a catastrophic change in the material conditions of existence of
the species – has sparked a veritable metaphysical anguish.
This anguish has expressed itself as a profound distrust of all
figures of anthropocentrism, be it as a Promethean ideology
of the progress of humankind toward a sociotechnical millennium, be it as the post-modern pessimism that ironically
celebrates the Subject's constituent power at the same time
as denouncing it as an inexhaustible source of illusions. The
awareness that the portentous project of "social construction of reality" realized itself as "capitalist destruction of
the planet" brings out a (near) consensus around the need
to declare as past – that is, to make pass – the *world of the
worldless people* that is (that was) the world of the Moderns.
Current transformations of this mythical scheme move in
different directions, however; some of them seek to invert
the negative sign that marks this destruction, advocating the
radical abolition of the world as the only way out toward
the final emancipatory transfiguration of the human. In an
age in which manic exuberance and melancholic depression
seem to fight over the helm of the collective psyche, every
discourse on the end of the world elicits an inverse discourse
preaching the perenniality of the human, its endless capacity for overcoming and sublimation, and tending to see any
mention to the ideas of decline or end as unreal, far-fetched,
reactionary, and superstitious.

The thanatological argument

Against this world of worldless people has arisen a certain
explicit will to the "renewal of metaphysics," also known as
the "ontological turn" in contemporary thought, a movement
or trend that includes philosophers whose name is more often
associated to the problematic known as "speculative realism,"
such as Ray Brassier, Iain Hamilton Grant, Graham Harman,
and Levi Bryant, as well as some others, like Quentin Meillassoux, Bruno Latour, and Tristan Garcia, who are sometimes
(more or less pertinently) claimed by the leading heads of
that movement.[3] Despite the far from negligible differences
among them, they all display a certain disposition to tackle

classic metaphysical questions head on, an anti-Kantian and anti-humanist bent of varying but unequivocal intensity, a pronounced indifference to the philosophy of language and a common "passion for the real." Some of them have devoted special attention to non-human beings, objects and quasi-objects, to materiality as a properly ontological dimension, to technology and the natural sciences; political philosophy and sociocultural anthropology are generally not the group's forte.[4]

What is of interest to us here is one particular aspect of speculative realism,[5] which we propose to see as a variant of the "world without us" mythical scheme; but a far more extreme variant than the mere imagining of a cosmos where the human species would be absent, as in Weisman's thought experiment.[6] The world without us that we are dealing with in this case is a world independent from all experience, prior to any actual or virtual description. A world without observers, defined essentially, and not just accidentally, by the absence of perspective. A world, in fact, that is radically dead.

This vision of the world as pure, a-subjective (or even anti-subjective), indifferent materiality is primarily sketched out in the works of Quentin Meillassoux and Ray Brassier. The former, in his influential *After Finitude*, originally published in French in 2006, proposes what he regards as the only speculative antidote to biblical creationism and, more generally, all religious worldviews that have come back to haunt the contemporary hegemony of the scientific image of reality. The intraphilosophical enemy that is the book's target, the one that would have made the fortress of Reason vulnerable to the fideist hordes, is what Meillassoux dubs *correlationism*; to wit, the affirmation of a reciprocal determination between thinking and being, "the idea according to which we only ever have access to the correlation between thinking and being, and never to either term considered apart from the other" (Meillassoux 2009: 5). Naturally, the culprit here is Kant, who allegedly led philosophy down a path distancing it infinitely from the "Great Outdoors" and trapping it inside the golden cage of the subject.[7] With Kant, in short, we have lost the world and turned inwards, in what could be described as a veritable psychotic episode in the history of our metaphysics: the modern constitutive subject is a narcissistic hallucination, and the legislating Understanding, a proverbial Napoleon in a provincial madhouse.

The problem with correlationism, according to its critics, is the primacy of the relation over its terms; it is necessary to separate Being from thought if we are to get to the rock bottom of the real, the world of extra-subjective primary qualities. It should be noted that what Meillassoux and the majority of speculative realists seem to be interested in is not both terms taken in isolation; it is the world or Being as external to thought that concerns them, not thought (language, society, culture, etc.) as such, of which Meillassoux has little more to say than that it can get hold of extra-experiential reality through mathematical means.[8]

Meillassoux identifies the correlationist position with Kantian transcendental idealism, phenomenology, postmodern skepticism, and other anti-absolutisms; but he sees it as equally present, in an even more virulent fashion, in all "subjectalist" philosophies that wish to absolutize or ontologize correlation (which had remained only epistemic or critical in classic correlationism and its descendants) – namely Hegel's objective idealism, Nietzsche's philosophy of the will, and the various discourses he incriminates as "hyperphysical," of a spiritualist, vitalist, or panpsychist inclination.[9] As Meillassoux understands it, the correlationist attitude entails relativism (this metaphysical Judas), and relativism subtracts the world from us, handing it over to "fideism" and irrationalism. Against these worldless people – correlationists and their Hegelian or Wittgensteinian, Heideggerian or Bergsonian progeny – Meillassoux defends the absolute preeminence of a world without people as the ultimate guarantee of any authentic materialism.

The thought experiment that he employs to sustain his metaphysical realism is oddly similar to Weisman's, though it is rhetorically turned here to realities that are *distant* in time and/or space. This is the "argument of ancestrality," addressing the truth status that we can (and contingently must) ascribe to statements describing states of affairs that we suppose (or know) to have occurred before the advent of the human species and its symbolic apparatus (language, culture, etc.).[10] Examples of such states of affairs are events like the origin of the universe, the formation of the solar system, the emergence of life on Earth, the appearance of the first species of the *Homo* genus, etc. These states of affairs generate what he calls "arche-fossils," material traces of realities and events that precede the advent of the human yet are nonetheless accessible to knowledge. The latter would prove the illegitimacy of the correlationist hypothesis and put an end to the shameful divorce between modern science, which bears witness to an effective access to a reality that is subject-independent, and modern philosophy, which insists in subordinating the thought of Being to the being of thought, or rather, the essentially non-being of thought.

The affirmation of the world's reality and of the subsistence of Being thus seems, for Meillassoux, to depend on a derealization of thought. And not only of human thought, or of thought's subject-form, but of all kinds of sentience or experience, human or non-human. It is life as sentience that must be excluded from reality's ultimate structure; any dependence of existence on experience must be denied. For Meillassoux, life in general and the human noosphere in particular are in effect the result of a radical *ex nihilo* emergence, a miracle without God (for the time being...).[11] They demonstrate a "superior absurdity of Time," which excludes from the world not only the principle of life but also the meaning of every principle, namely, the principle of sufficient reason. Only the principle of non-contradiction, necessary for the affirmation of the necessity of contingency, remains in place. This is why it seems to us, if the wordplay can be pardoned, that it is not contingent that Time (with a capital T) is anointed by Meillassoux as Lord of the Absurd: the end of the world here becomes both imminent (as there is no reason whatsoever why it would not end a second from now) and insignificant.

The world-without-us advanced by Ray Brassier, to whose dense and complex *Nihil Unbound* we shall make no more than an allusion here, is, like Weisman's, situated in the future, only this future is as remote as Meillassoux's ancestral world, a "cosmological deep time"[12] in decisive contrast with correlationism's "anthropological time." The empirical fact that sets Brassier's hyper-nihilist argument in motion is the inexorable annihilation of our species, life, planet, and universe. In the long run, as the saying goes, we are all dead;

but this means for Brassier (2007: 119) that we are all *already* dead, or rather, that "*everything* is dead already." More than derealizing thought in order to affirm Being, according to Brassier the task is to annihilate it, eliminating it not only from the future but sempiternally – thought is "radically devalue[d] in the present" (Shaviro 2011), being excluded from Being, which radically exceeds it, *in toto*. At the same time, the subject of thought, the physical or metaphysical position of a "we," is rendered epiphenomenal and as inert as matter. For the author, it is necessary to extinguish sense, radicalizing the disenchantment of the world initiated by the Enlightenment, in order to "clear the way for the intelligibility of extinction. Senselessness and purposelessness are not merely privative; they represent a gain in intelligibility" (Brassier 2007: 238). Whereas for Meillassoux there is no principle of reason, for Brassier reason has no principles; but intelligibility still is, he judges, a better (non-)bliss than ignorance.

The importance and frequency of the word "death" in Meillassoux's and Brassier's writings is worth remarking upon. Meillassoux (2012) speaks of "dead existence" and "dead matter" as the ultimate substance of the cosmos, on which the phenomena of life and thought supervene metaphysically *ex nihilo*, as realities that have no bearing on the universe's inorganic substrate. Brassier, in turn, makes abundant use of Freud's death drive as a cosmological principle, identifying a thanatological tropism ("thanatropism") in life and thought. The emancipatory potential of this fatal attraction – emancipatory for humans, it is understood; other living beings were not consulted – is something that should be politically stimulated; Brassier's nihilism is a militant stance, not a quietistic one.

Whereas in Weisman's thought experiment and in the Edenic motifs of a world-without-us the operative distinction was the one between *life* and *humanity*, in the antianthropocentric scheme of this strain of speculative realism the opposition would rather be that between *life* (human and non-human) and *world*, understood as substantive reality or the matter of Being. It is necessary to deny life as an activity of sentience and signification in order to affirm Being's autonomous truth as "in-itselfness." The Great Outdoors is a glacial wasteland, radical exteriority is absolutely, outlandishly *dead*. One could say that, for these thinkers, to speak of an "end of the world," far from a pragmatic contradiction (as Chakrabarty suggests is the case with Weisman), is, on the contrary, a sheer metaphysical tautology, a trivial ontological pleonasm: the end is the world's mode of "existence."

We tend to agree with Shaviro (2011) when he points out how Meillassoux's and Brassier's presupposition that matter, if it is to exist in itself (outside correlation), must be passive and inert – in the sense of insentient, indifferent, and meaningless – reintroduces the human exceptionalism that it purported to eliminate. The anti-anthropocentric decision at the root of these two versions of the "world without us" theme reveals itself to be, when all is said and done, obsessed with the human point of view. It is as if the negation of this point of view were a necessary condition for the world to exist – a curious negative idealism, a weird cadaverous subjectalism. (The broader anti-vitalism defended by these authors, which grounds this anti-anthropocentrism, comes across above all as a pre-emptive, precautionary measure to ensure the neutralization of what really bothers them, to wit, life "as we know it" from the inside – human experience, which ends up overvalued by the very care taken to invalidate it.) But a negative anthropocentrism is still an anthropocentrism – perhaps the only really radical one – as much as those who burned idols were the only fetishists in the grotesque comedy of errors of colonialism, since they truly believed in the unreality of fetishes in the same way that they (unrealistically) believed that "savages" truly believed in their reality (Latour 2010a).

Finally, it seems to us that establishing a *maximal* discontinuity between a sublunar or terrestrial perspective and a supralunar or cosmic one is essential for these two versions of the world-without-us, as both assume a "bifurcation of nature," in Whitehead's sense.[13] Ennis (2013) highlights the opposition between Brassier's "noir" cosmocentrism and the "relativistic" geocentrism of so-called continental philosophy, epitomized in Husserl's originary ark, Heidegger's fourfold, or the Earth (the great Deterritorialized) in Deleuze and Guattari – to which we could add, of course, the Gaia (or Gaias) of Latour and Stengers. But this rift between the cosmological and anthropological orders, between a cosmological deep-time and a human-historical time – which thus repeats the obsolete distinction between Nature and Culture in the very same gesture that affirms the all-encompassing pre-eminence of dead Nature over something that "should not be there" (experience) – is precisely what is being *empirically* contested by the collapse of scales and strata of planetary reality, that is, by the metamorphosis of the human species into a major geophysical agent. When we displace the problematic of anti-correlationism to the "ecological" plane of the sublunar, formulating the question of the relation between thought and Being in terms of humankind and world and thus reducing the distance between reality as Universe and reality as Gaia, we can see the irony of our current predicament as that of a catastrophic *terrestrial objectivation of the correlation*. That is, the fact that human thought, materialized as a giant technological machine of planetary impact, effectively and destructively *correlates the world*, burying the arche-fossils of the remote past under thick layers of anthropocenic soil – concrete, plastic, tarmac – (Söllin and Warde 2011; Pálsson et al. 2013: 5), rich with what will be the anthropofossils of a future perhaps not so far away. The anti-correlationism of Meillassoux and other materialist metaphysicians of his generation therefore sounds, probably against their explicit intentions, as a pathetic cry of protest, if not a magical formula of exorcism or disavowal, against the forebodingly *realizing* power of thought, at least in our humble terrestrial abode.

"Nobody will miss it"

It does not strike us as inappropriate to compare Brassier's militant nihilism and similar philosophical arguments regarding the end of the world and of thought to those scenarios projected by films such as Lars von Trier's *Melancholia* and Abel Ferrara's *4:44 Last Day on Earth*, which imagine an instantaneous end of all terrestrial life – or universal life, in von Trier's case.

Melancholia portrays the collision of our world with the absolute Outside, materialized as the planet Melancholia – a gigantic "blue planet" like ours, which unexpectedly emerges from the depths of the cosmos to cross Earth's path. The film stages the contrast between the human world, with its interminable melodramas and contradictions (family, work, the wedding party, the magnificent upper-class country estate, silent class war), and the cosmos-without-us, the austere ballet of the spheres that evolves in all its sublimity in long shots of the solar system and beyond. Apart from a few elements that suggest possible mediations between the two dimensions, they appear incommunicable until their fatal encounter.[14] John, the scientist brother-in-law, who possesses the only instrument capable of providing objective access to the outside world, chooses to commit suicide when he discovers his science to be fallible and powerless. In the same way that he dies inside his beautiful property, none of the other main characters – horses included – seem capable of crossing the brook that borders the estate. There is no way out.[15]

Perhaps more than in any other disaster movie in the history of cinema, the destruction represented in *Melancholia* is not simply an episode of crisis or the interruption (by death) of the course of life in the tale of a group of human individuals (the sinking of a transatlantic, the fire in a skyscraper), an accident situated within the history of Western civilization more broadly (the end of the United States, for instance), or even a parable on the extinction of *Homo sapiens* pure and simple, but a presentation of *the end of the end*. The clash with planet Melancholia is the event to end all events, and time itself, in the same sense in which Anders referred to nuclear apocalypse: *no one* is left, there is no offscreen voice to comment on the end of the world. Real time disappears to the point that it is impossible even to imagine the verbal tense in which to narrate what cannot be narrated apart from a mute "present" (no one is left, there is no voice). The impact is followed by darkness or, rather, a black screen, the pure absence of images, silence, nothingness. The end of the world is the end of the film, and the end of the film is the end of the world (Szendy 2015).

Of all the characters in the film, the melancholic Justine is the only one who *"knows things"* (but knows them in a different way from her scientist brother-in-law, John). It is she who from the start peers into the starry sky and realizes something is wrong; she is also the one for whom the prospect of the disaster will be easiest to accept. Hers are the film's harshest words: the end of life on Earth is the end of all life in the universe, but that is no reason for sorrow.

> *Justine:* The earth is evil. We don't need to grieve for it.
> *Claire:* What?
> *Justine:* Nobody will miss it.
> *Claire:* But where would Leo grow?
> *Justine:* All I know is, life on earth is evil.
> *Claire:* There may be life somewhere else.
> *Justine:* But there isn't.

Her disphoria is ontological and absolute, independent from a circumstantial, outside motive, and thus very different, also in that respect, from the despair that will take hold of Claire. Nevertheless, in the very last seconds before the Encounter, already inside the "magic cave," the simulacrum of an indigenous teepee that she builds with her nephew, we see the melancholia in her face give way to what seems to us a crease of fear.[16] A mere reflex contraction, perhaps, but precisely for that reason an (un)equivocal *sign of life*. It is just this moment of fear and shock that seems to differentiate *Melancholia* from the apocalypse announced by Brassier. Let us remember that, before bringing the end of the world, the catastrophe is, precisely, a clash or shock, that is, an Encounter and an Event, and that, between the perspective of an imminent end and the end itself, there are a few seconds of maximally intense affect. It is not just in order to relieve Claire's despair and Leo's alarm that Justine helps the latter build the tepee's spindly frame of dry boughs. The "magical cave," without material walls, might not be an escape, as there is nowhere to run to, but it is a way out or a line of flight found by the characters to meet the Event and transcendentally counter-effectuate it, in those few seconds of hyperconcentrated thought.[17]

Brassier's "truth of extinction" is deduced from what is taken today as a scientific projection (rather than a traditional mythical prophecy) of the macrocosmic event that will put an end not only the world-Earth, but to the whole world-universe, some trillions of years from now. It is only when this truth travels back into the past, in a "thanatropic regression"[18] *of thought* that takes infinitely less time than those trillions of years into the future, that the philosopher's discourse arrives at the meaninglessness of our present life. Like Brassier, Shaviro, in his analysis of *Melancholia* – even while he mentions climate change in passing as an event that reminds *us* of the autonomy of the world-without-us, the chaos underlying the cosmos[19] – seems to move too quickly from the human world (the all-too-human history of capitalism) to this cosmic, or rather chaotic, world. Could this be the reason why he repeats so many times in his analysis of *Melancholia* that Lars Von Trier's film is, unlike most disaster movies, "deflationary," and that the vision of the cosmos and the clash itself leave us indifferent, except maybe for the aesthetic pleasure we feel in observing all those beautiful and remote images? To the present authors, and it seems also to Peter Szendy (2015), the last scenes are, on the contrary, utterly terrifying. This is also maybe why, in "Against Self-Organization," Shaviro (2009) shows himself sympathetic to the "Medea hypothesis" advanced by biologist Peter Ward, who offered it as an alternative to James Lovelock's Gaia Theory. According to Ward's (2009) hypothesis, the history of life and mass extinctions on Earth demonstrates that vital processes have effects on the environment that are destabilizing rather than homeostatic. "[L]ife on Earth is doomed to extinction long before the heating and expansion of the sun make the Earth too hot to live on," Shaviro (2009) summarizes. We should bear in mind, however, that what led Lovelock to Gaia was precisely the incongruity and fragility of this niche of negentropy that is living Earth – which can of course cease to exist in its present form at any moment. As Latour maliciously recounts the story in his magnificent third Gifford Lecture, Lovelock places himself in a point of view outside the Earth and, looking back at it, sees something that was not supposed to be there (here), something like a cosmological *hapax*: the stabilization of terrestrial atmosphere with enormously unlikely concentrations of certain gases fundamental to life.

It is precisely because life is here, even though it "should not" be, that climate change is also an event-for-us. It has, as we have argued, following Chakrabarty, collapsed together the three histories that once seemed as distinct and discrete as the two worlds in *Melancholia*: the histories of the Earth, of life on Earth, and "ours." This, we think, is why Justine feels afraid, even though she knows the catastrophe has already happened.

5

Alone at last

This is the way the world ends
This is the way the world ends
This is the way the world ends
Not with a bang but a whimper.
                                    T. S. Eliot

Ceci n'est pas un monde

Von Trier's aesthetico-philosophical experiment evidently
suffers from a lack of "realism." It is unlikely that a cosmic
or even ecological Armageddon could come so abruptly and
at such short notice to put an end to our form of life. The
film's allegorical truth lies instead in the suddenness (at the
scale of the species' biography) of our awareness of Gaia's
intrusion, and the rapidly growing conviction of the irreversibility of this intrusion: Gaia has come to stay, and it will
change our lives forever (Stengers 2015: 47).[1] For that reason,
Gaia resembles planet Melancholia much more than it does
the Earth. Melancholia is an image of the titanic, enigmatic
transcendence of Gaia, an entity that suddenly and devastat-
ingly falls on a world, ours, that has suddenly become *all
too human*.

   Abel Ferrara's *4:44 Last Day on Earth*, while it is the most
"verisimilar" of all recent apocalyptic films, in its portrait

of the chaotic Babel that is humankind's rising awareness of
the dangers of anthropogenic climate change, on the other
hand, like *Melancholia*, incurs in the same gesture of con-
densing all the complexity and "hyperobjectivity" of climate
change and environmental degradation into a single event, in
this case a planetary conflagration unleashed by the sudden
disappearance of the ozone layer, with a set time to happen
(4:44 sharp).[2] But there is no cosmic point of view here.
The whole world that ends is seen from inside "our" world,
the pathetically, trivially, uninterestingly human world of the
bohemian Lower East Side in New York City (or, at most,
whatever information arrives there, via Skype or TV, of the
preparations with which distant populations await the final
hour). We have to make an effort to identify the non-human
elements of this world about to end all at once – a tree being
felled, a dog patiently waiting to be fed by its owner in what
looks like a last meal.

But the world might also fade away little by little instead.
The prospect of planetary environmental crisis seems to offer
not so much the risk of sudden death as that of an aggravat-
ing degenerative disease, the insidious onset of which had
originally escaped us. If business remains as usual, the most
verisimilar narrative tells us that we (or those of us who are
left) will all effectively live in ever worsening conditions,
in a world ever more similar to Philip K. Dick's dystopian
gnosis.[3] Worlds (or "pseudo-worlds," as Dick explains) in
which space and time start to rot and to disintegrate, where
actions are interrupted and follow incomprehensible courses,
where effects erratically precede their causes, hallucinations
become materialized in contradictory ontologies, life and
death become technologically indiscernible; where elusive
hypercapitalist Messiahs run media-based religions for the
poor masses neutered by mood-enhancing devices; where
trying to retain one's lucidity is the characters' only possible
(and ultimately impossible) occupation, amidst an entropy
that corrodes the narrative itself and plays havoc with diegetic
logic. Dick's books do not so much *describe* as they *inscribe*
the shattering of the real. As Leibniz argued when exposing
the pyramidal scheme of possible worlds at the end of his
Theodicy, there is an infinite number of worlds worse than
any one we can be in. The worst possible world does not

exist, but there is only one best possible world; sadly, it is ours. In Leibniz's time, this could still be taken for optimism.[4]

There is no dearth of examples in recent literature and in cinema of pessimistic representations (even if in a some-times celebratory mode) of a future corresponding to the "us-without-world" scheme, that is, a humanity from which the fundamental conditions of existence have been sub-tracted. *Mad Max* is the first to come to mind, but we could equally refer to *The Matrix*, if we accept a certain equivalence between the world as ecological desert of the first film and the world made up of mirages of the second – an ensemble of simulacra arising, as we know, from "the desert of real."[5] In both cases, we are faced with an "end of the world" in the sense of a specifically *human* world, its end resulting from a process of ontological devitalization of the environment (the planet's total devastation or artificialization) with "dehuman-izing" effects over the surviving humankind.

But maybe the best example of a worldless humanity sce-nario is Cormac McCarthy's novel *The Road*, in which the author's terse style and the gloomy theme harmonize to per-fection. The apocalyptic myth developed there can be sum-marized in a simple formula: there will be nothing in the end, just human beings – and not for long. The book tells the story of a father and a son's journey across a dark, dead, putrid land in the wake of a global environmental disaster of indeterminate causes. With all ecosystems laid to waste, without animals, plants, or drinking water, the few humans left behind lead a sordid existence living off the remains of civilization (canned food, clothes, and tools gathered from department stores) or engaging in cannibalism.

The Road describes the unfolding of an inexorable, accel-erating process of decay that reminds us somewhat of Philip K. Dick's (1983) *Ubik*, in which objects grow old faster and faster, until we finally realize that death is not, as we thought, an external enemy against which we fight a hugely asym-metrical war, but an internal enemy: we are already dead and life is what has passed into the outside.[6] We can say that there is something here like an exchange of perspectives in the Amerindian sense: while we thought of ourselves as defending the world of the living, we had long been captured by the point of view of the dead.[7] ("We are already dead!" is also the sentence screamed at the top of his lungs by Willem Dafoe's character in 4:44, to those who, in a vain attempt to exercise their free will for the last time in the face of imminent death, start committing suicide by throwing themselves out of the windows of their flats. Despite its stentorious power, that cry is ultimately more like the whining whimper in Eliot's poem.) In McCarthy's novel, in fact, death threatens to capture the few living beings that remain by subtracting the world from them: denying them objects, eroding their human memory, and gradually corroding language itself; ravaging their bodies with disease and hunger; transforming them into the fodder of cannibal predators, ex-humans who have lost their souls, that is, their *humanity*, precisely. Aphasia preludes anthropophagy.[8] It is hard to read this book without the distressing sensation that we already live in the world of the dead, and that the metaphorical "fire" that some characters still carry is no more than a half-life, like the one that the recently deceased retain in *Ubik*, soon to be extinguished. The whole world is dead, and we are inside it. The boy's father dies; the boy travels on with people he met on the road, and who appear to be trustworthy. But they have nowhere to go. Those who journey down the road will come to no place, for the simple reason that there is no place left to come to. There is no way out.

Another example of a world that hollows out little by little, leaving humans entirely defenseless, is Béla Tarr's and Ágnes Hranitzky's magnificent *The Turin Horse* (2011, the same year as *Melancholia*). The protagonists here are not a twosome, as in *The Road* and 4:44, but three: a partially invalid old man, his adult daughter, and the family's draft horse (the "same" horse, somehow, that initiated Nietzsche's breakdown in Turin). They live in a minuscule, destitute farm in the middle of a windswept steppe. The end of the world of Tarr's poor peasants is a withering away rather than a rotting out. It is the dry, sterile wind that howls continuously, blowing dead leaves and dust; it is the water well gone dry; it is the light that goes out for lack of fuel; it is the horse that inexplicably stops eating (the horse as an apocalyptic beast, as in *Melancholia*); it is the creeping dying away of communication between father and daughter, who little by little cease to talk to or even look at each other, preferring

to contemplate, static and silent, the parched world that sur-
rounds them. It is above all the naked, useless, blind, and
machine-like repetition of everyday actions that progressively
grinds the characters down. First the horse, then the old
man and his daughter, the two of whom end up motionless,
slumped round the table in their dark hut, their unchanging
meal in front of them – two potatoes, one each, now no
longer cooked due to lack of fire and water, which remain
untouched as the film fades out. As in *Melancholia* (and
again Buñuel's *The Exterminating Angel*), the theme of the
failed attempt to escape, to break free from the magic circle
of depression, signals a tipping point of (in)action. When the
well dries out, the characters pull the exhausted horse and
the cart to the nearby village – "wrecked by the joint work of
men and God," as a neighbor who drops in to buy spirits says
to them: "We destroyed the world, and it's also God's fault."
Yet they inexplicably come back after a few minutes (hours?
days?), giving in for good to an all-embracing paralysis – the
old man has a paralyzed arm from the start of the film – and
worn down by a world that is itself catatonic.

The Turin Horse can be seen as developing a cosmological equivalent of the theme of the banality of evil. For Tarr,
rather than a Dantean spectacle, the end of the world[9] will
be a fractal, incremental decay, a disappearance that is slow
and imperceptible, and yet so complete it can make itself
disappear before our eyes that gradually go blind:

> The apocalypse is a huge event. But reality is not like that. In
> my film, the end of the world is very silent, very weak. So the
> end of the world comes as I see it coming in real life – slowly
> and quietly. Death is always the most terrible scene, and when
> you watch someone dying – an animal or a human – it's
> always terrible, and the most terrible thing is that it looks like
> nothing happened. (Tarr 2011)

Nothing happened – we are just dead.

After the future: the end as beginning

There are those who nonetheless view the prospect of losing
the world with enthusiasm; no more than the casting aside

of a provisional, no longer necessary scaffolding, the end of the world, as the end of non-human or anti-human "Nature," will effectively be the fulfillment of human destiny. The species' technological genius will make it capable of living in an *Umwelt* made to order *for* and *by* humankind. It is this literally *constructivist* version of worldless humanity that informs the vision of a coming leap forward, a stepped-up progress that will liberate human beings – maybe just the 1 percent to begin with? – from their "biological substrate," extending the longevity of individuals at first, and finally attaining the transcendence of organic corporeality altogether (our "wetware," to borrow from Rudy Rucker).

The project of self-fabrication of future man and his environment through eugenics and the technological synthesis of a new Nature is promoted by the advocates of the Singularity thesis, prominent among whom are pop thinkers situated on the borders of technology (in the double sense of technical mastery and technological thought) and science fiction, such as Vernon Vinge and Ray Kurzweil.[10] "Singularity" names a radical anthropological discontinuity, a sudden cybernetic Rapture that is being prepared as we speak by the exponential increase in processing capacity of the global computer network. Some twenty years or so from now, this increase will arrive at a catastrophic point of inflection (think Teilhard de Chardin's "Omega point"), when it will finally surpass the collective capacity of all grey matter in the planet. Human biology and technology will come into fusion with one another, generating a superior form of machinic consciousness that will nonetheless still be at the service of the human will – enabling, in particular, the transmigration of souls, that is, the codification of consciousness into software that can be run in an indefinite number of material platforms, uploadable onto the computer network so as to be available for posterior reincarnation in bodies that are purely synthetic, or genetically engineered to the minutest detail. Death, to whom we owe the very idea of necessity, will have become optional at last.

This variant of the "worldless humans" scheme, understood here as the overcoming of the species' organic or earthly condition, expresses a belief in, and above all the desire for, a technological development that can lead us inexorably, though it can be bravely accelerated or cowardly retarded, toward an essential enhancement of Man: a *übermenschlich* state or New Age in which "we" will have definitively and literally become the world-makers dear to Heidegger – though, ironically, that will have been achieved through technical means. The culmination of the Anthropocene brings with it the obsolescence of the human, but in an "upwardly mobile" sense, as its glorious transfiguration: come the Kingdom of Man, worldliness will be absorbed by a technically magnified humankind emancipated from the world. We will no longer be accountable to the world, we will no longer have to deal with any limits, because we will have become the world by turning the world itself – the cosmos as a whole – into a "magnificently sublime form of intelligence" (Kurzweil 2005: 21).[11] *Homo universus*. In the future, in short, everything will be human. Or, the more malicious among us might suggest, everything will be Californian.[12]

Singularitarians, as they are called, do not seem to worry too much about whether the parameters of the Earth System will be sufficiently generous to grant us enough time for the leap ahead. The environmental crisis already in place does not enter their calculations, or figures in them as already solved in advance by the imminent arrival of technological Rapture and human self-mutagenesis. Certain close relatives of the Singularitarian people, nevertheless, have devoted some attention to the problem, inquiring into the immediate technological conditions for the survival of capitalism and its main conquests, liberty and security, in a situation of growing energy consumption and persistent dependence on fossil fuels. The Breakthrough Institute, a think tank from North America (California, in fact) whose exact position on the political spectrum is hard to pinpoint,[13] is perhaps the most visible name among the advocates of a green capitalism that puts its faith on centralized solutions that would be capable of implementing ambitious techno-engineering projects on behalf of big capital, with high material investment and organically (if that is the right word) embedded in Big Science: hydraulic fracking of rock to obtain fossil fuels, expanding and perfecting nuclear power stations, large hydroelectric projects (like the dams in the Amazon Basin),

generalizing the monoculture of genetically modified vegetables, environmental geo-engineering, and so on.

Ted Nordhaus and Michael Shellenbenger, the institute's
two founders and authors of the award-winning *Break
Through: From the Death of Environmentalism to the Politics of Possibility* (2009, first published in 2007), provide a
good example of this current that Patrick Curry (2011) has
called "cornucopian technophiles."[14] The book is a piece of
advertisement for a "vibrant postindustrial capitalism" (Nordhaus and Shellenberger 2009: 249) able to sustain without
much effort the 10 billion people that will inhabit the Earth
by the middle of this century. "Big is beautiful": this watchword, first launched by the authors in a lecture at the Yale
School of Forestry and Environmental Studies (Nordhaus and
Shellenberger 2011), is provided with justification in a chapter
of *Break Through* appropriately entitled "Greatness." There,
Nordhaus and Shellenberger develop, say, an inventive
reading of Nietzsche, in particular of his call for the creation
of values adequate to our times with which to replace philosophies of *ressentiment*, pessimism, and limits with a "philosophy of gratitude, overcoming, and possibility" (2009:
248). From this highly unlikely marriage of Nietzsche and
Pollyanna, a eugenically monstrous daughter is born, an ecopolitical Barbie that we could christen Gratitude of the Rich:

> Those of us who are fortunate enough to have met our basic
> material and postmaterial needs should feel neither guilt nor
> shame at our wealth, freedom, and privilege, but rather *grati-
> tude*. Whereas guilt drives us to deny our wealth, gratitude
> inspires us to share it. It is gratitude, not guilt, that will moti-
> vate Americans to embrace the aspirations of others to become
> wealthy, free, and fortunate as we are. (Ibid.: 249–50)

If this sounds less like a properly Nietzschean thesis than
a tele-evangelist sanctimoniously announcing to his sheep the
prosperity that awaits them, it is probably because it is. In the
authors' vision, degrowth theoreticians, environmentalists
who dare talk about the need to reduce consumption, scientists that insist on the idea of planetary biogeophysical limits,
and all other such Cassandras trade on a toxic combination
of Malthusian pettiness, metaphysical nihilism, and historical

bad conscience. In short, they represent a constellation of "reactive forces" that deny the planet's peoples – only human peoples count here, needless to say – the life of abundance that is our Destiny.[15] The problem with environmentalists, say Nordhaus and Shellenberger (2009: 127), is their lack of imagination: they should have "imagined" that the solution for global warming resides not in the restriction but the liberation of economic activity and technological development. Instead of scaling down, we need to scale up even more, produce, innovate, grow, and prosper, so we can finally bring that abundance to those who are presently excluded from it. In other words: we must let the cake rise before we can share it, and we should even *accelerate* its rise.[16]

Rather than the catastrophic singularity prophesized by the visionary vanguard of Californian futurology, the Breakthrough Institute does not imagine any dramatic breakthroughs will take place. Its founders, on the contrary, believe in continuous progress, a "modernization of modernization" as Ulrich Beck might say: a perfectioning of the technical apparatus of capitalist civilization until the latter can absorb – or, even better, render productive – the destructive consequences that it sows along its path. (To put it differently: so it can reap generous profits with that technical *Aufhebung*.) The scheme projected by the Breakthrough Institute's ideology can thus be seen as a variant of the mythical theme of a "humanity without world," in the sense that, in the "good Anthropocene" to come, there will no longer be an environment that is *external* (read: hostile) to humankind. Not so much because man will be transfigured by technology, as Singularitarians dream, but because the old Nature will be recodified (or rather re-axiomatized) by the capitalist machine as merely a matter of managing resources, of *environmental governance* – everything according to so-called "best practice." The anthropic dream of the Moderns would thus be finally materialized: a post-environmentalism in which man will find himself contextualized and sustained only by himself, surrounded by the immense accumulation of commodities, energized by his shiny new and super-safe nuclear centrals (with cold-fusion reactors, if possible), and relaxed by large and pleasant ecological leisure areas, populated of course by a carefully curated, genetically enhanced flora.[17]

The cosmologies of Singularitarianism and of the Breakthrough Institute rank alongside the gospels of capitalist
re-enchantment, to the extent that they announce an internal
mutation of the present economic system, when the productive
forces of hypermodernity will generate an ecopolitical order
founded on humankind's universal access (that is the promise,
at least) to the new material abundance. But there is a curious
left-wing variant of Singularitarian-cornucopian eschatology
which has received a fair amount of attention lately, going by
the name of "accelerationism" – an ironic label at first, later
to be reclaimed by its partisans. Accelerationist theoreticians,
the vast majority of which hail from or live in Old Europe,
generally boast a sophisticated metaphysical disenchantment
sometimes bordering on what Deleuze and Guattari (1987:
229) would call a "passion for abolition," going as far as
the eulogy of a certain necrophiliac *jouissance*. This attitude
inscribes itself in the horizon of a paroxystic intensification
of the new spirit of capitalism that (it is hoped) could lead
to a radical technopolitical rupture resulting in the structural
transformation of relations of production. If Singularitarians
are possessed by a geekish technological optimism, accelerationists align themselves with the aesthetics and politics of
cyberpunk, haughtily affirming the power of the negative and
sometimes displaying a strong nostalgia for the Soviet version
of the modernization front.

§ Benjamin Noys (2008, 2014) coined the term "accelerationism," mapped the movement's cultural references (1980s science
fiction, Black Metal, Donna Haraway's "Cyborg Manifesto,"
and Italian post-workerism, among others), and traced its philosophical genealogy. The latter would date back at least to certain
texts by Deleuze and Guattari, Lyotard, and Baudrillard as rein-
terpreted by the charismatic (but also quasi-delirious and, for
some, frankly embarrassing) figure of Nick Land. A lecturer at
Warwick University in the 1990s, Land was the mentor of two
of the leading figures of speculative realism, Ray Brassier and
Iain Hamilton Grant, as well as of an influential techno-Marxist
blogger, Mark Fisher (k-punk). His work bears many points
of contact with Californian Singularitarianism, but his futurology, apart from being far richer in philosophical references, is
profoundly "gothic" or "Luciferian" (Williams 2011). In one
of his better-known texts, "Meltdown," Land (2011) alludes

to a growing compression of temporal crisis cycles allegedly converging upon a coming "terrestrial meltdown singularity" (Mackay 2012). In a more recent work, Noys (2014) offers an inspired analysis of accelerationism's antecedents as well as the movement's sharpest internal critique, since he shares some of the premises of the authors he criticizes.

The accelerationists' basic intuition is that a certain world, which has already ended, must *finish ending*, that is, fully actualize its inexistence. This world that others (the usual *ingénues*, dreamers, tree-huggers, hippies) imagined existed in all its idyllic splendor before the advent of capitalism, and which according to the latter would subsist today in a diminished, downtrodden way, suffocated by the smoke of dark satanic mills, is but a romantic illusion, a retro matrix that distorts the perception of the really existing present world. For the real world is *this*, our deserted world of late capitalism, in which the "Second Nature" of political economy exercises its uncontested metaphysical – if not physical – sovereignty over "First Nature," the old *physis* that is always too ecological, organic, and vitalistic.[18] Real subsumption has spread universally, the capitalist system has become absolutely hegemonic, its capacity to absorb any resistance seemingly unlimited, reality having become a derisory corollary of its own simulacrum. There is no more – and so there never will have been – an "outside" of capitalism, an exterior that would be anterior to it, a wilderness beyond its history, an archaic concrescence that it would not have already vaporized with its implacable incandescence: all that is solid, etc. Thus, the only way to conjure an Outside is to produce it from the inside by driving the capitalist machine into overdrive, to accelerate the acceleration that defines it, to maximize the creative destruction that moves it until it finishes by destroying itself and creating for us a radically *new* world. After the apocalypse, the Kingdom.

As for the humanity that inhabits this universe-world without windows of late capitalism, it has not been human for a very long time. Far from imagining a "hot" (trans) humanization of the cosmos, accelerationists profess a "cold" post-humanism that acknowledges the a-subjectifying *de-hominization* of Man by deterritorialized technocapitalism, welcoming a "technological infiltration of human agency" capable of inducing changes in the species' cerebral anatomy and ultimately of dissolving the old provincialism of anthropic Culture into a new Nature that is cosmic, austere and sterile, chaotic and rarefied, impersonal and elemental.[19] The worker qua cognitive machine plugged into the Web, zombified by the continuous administration of chemical and semiotic drugs, the permanently indebted "prosumer" of the Immaterial, avidly enjoying its own exploitation, is the new heroic anti-subject of this jubilant dystopia of a frenetically devitalized post-world.

§ In several contemporary representations of the worldless people of the future we find the macabre figure of the zombie, which combines multiplicity and impersonality, cannibal omophagy and putrefaction. As we have seen, there was in *The Road* a double struggle, against the decomposition of the world into grey toxic mud on the one hand, and against the zombification of man on the other, a process embodied in the bands of faceless cannibals who feed on the weakest survivors (those that have not yet become completely dehumanized). In *Übik*, we discover as the story unfolds that the accelerated decay of those who find themselves in the twilight zone of "half-life" is due to the force exercised upon them by a single character, Jory (dead as a child and now also in half-life), who literally devours other people's half-lives, which take place in a reality mentally constructed by him in its minutest details. Finally, the protagonists of *The Turin Horse* seem to feed on a substance that does not nourish them, becoming progressively devitalized until they no longer "function," as if they had been eaten from the inside and nothing but the empty shell of their bodies continued to exist in a world that has itself been hollowed out. For an analysis of zombies, vampires, and cannibals in the contemporary imaginary, see Nodari and Cera (2013).

Accelerationism is one of the contemporary incarnations of a (broadly construed) Marxist philosophy of history. It gained momentum with the crises of 1968, 1989, 2001, 2008, and other emblematic dates of the successive "ends of the past" whose ominous or heartening signs have acted as milestones orienting the left's discourse on the "beginning of the future."[20] That lineage would mark it out as an anti-capitalist position in principle, but "post-" ultimately seems to be the prefix most adequate to it, given its resolutely teleological and unilinear vision of human history (Noys 2012) as well as, we might add, its virulent hostility to the particular version of the end of the past associated with the utopian convulsion of 1968.

Accelerationism usually claims the title of legitimate heir to the spirit of the left, focusing its polemical energies on battling alternative anti-capitalist positions – its taste for infighting being one sense at least in which it truly is an authentic heir to that spirit. Its major ideological enemy seems to be environmentalism and other such "reterritorializing" discourses (Lindblom 2012), whose dream it would be to return to less artificial conditions of existence, supposedly more faithful to the ontological indiscernibility between species, life, and world (continuity, horizontality, material correlation). According to the accelerationists, any defense of grabbing for the emergency brake to stop the runaway locomotive of capitalist growth would be a thinly disguised attempt at rescuing values and relations from the pre-capitalist past; a past not only unrecoverable, but both entirely imaginary and ultimately sordid. What worker today would wish to return to the "organic mud" of his ancestors? That is the question Mark Fisher (2014: 339) asks bitterly.

§ On the subject of returning to organic mud, one should recall the slogan of the squatters who, coming from several different parts of France and Europe, have joined the local farmers who refuse to sell their land in occupying the area that was earmarked by the French government to receive the "Great Western airport" in Notre-Dame-des-Landes, near Nantes, in Brittany. The slogan, which can be seen in the various barricades that interrupt and color the roads of the ZAD (*Zone à Defendre* or "Zone To Be Defended"), reads "we are the mud people" ("*nous sommes le peuple de boue*"). It is a play on words that sounds exactly like "we are the people standing up" ("*nous sommes le peuple débout*") – the risen people, the people up in arms, with their feet firmly planted on the ground (the region becomes very muddy with the winter rains) but their spine unbowed and their head held high. The occupation began in 2008 and has resisted until this day, having managed to subtract from state control an area of almost 2,000 ha under the heavy-handed repression of a French Republic willing to make full use of its most modern instruments of "legitimate violence" (riot police, tear gas and stun grenades, rubber bullets, juridical terrorism, etc.). The ZAD occupation in Notre-Dame-des-Landes is but one example of several "reclaim the land" movements that are emerging and connecting to each other all over the world. They seem to indicate that what is at stake is not so much a *return* to some "ancestral" mud as a *discovery* (which is also an "uncovering," in the sense of breaking up the tarmac, for example) of the Earth's surface and a *revelation* of its telluric potentials, inventing a *future* in which to toil in the mud will mean neither to prostrate oneself before a Lord nor to bow down before a Sovereign.[21]

Two young authors, Alex Williams and Nick Srnicek (2013), have recently published an "Accelerationist Manifesto" that is more solar, but no less caustic, than Nick Land's *fin-de-siècle* nihilistic alternative. The manifesto has done the rounds in the philosophical blogosphere, the Web being the ecological niche par excellence of speculative realists. The text defends a "Promethean politics of maximal mastery over society and its environment" as the only way to defeat capital.[22] This mastery aims to "preserve the gains of late capitalism" while avoiding the destruction of "the material platform of neoliberalism" (Ibid.). In short, it is a matter of "unleashing" the productive forces that capitalism, according to Marx and Engel's famous diagnosis, at once mobilizes and holds back, elicits and restricts. To do so, however, it is imperative that we once again put our faith in the Plan (read, the State), rediscovering a positive sense of transcendence that our simple-minded belief in the immanent virtues of the Web (read, the Market) had led us to despise. Central economic planning and vertical political authority thus win back their citizenship rights in the imaginary of a left without complexes, at ease in the messianic ambiance of Modernism. Some could also say: in the confused imagination of a left under the grip of a serious bout of Stockholm syndrome.

Like the Breakthrough Institute, with whom they share, if not the same faith in the regenerative powers of capitalism, at least the same hope in progress, accelerationists fault the existing left – or, more precisely, whatever remains of the spirit of '68 in whatever remains of the left – for a "staggering lack of imagination." (Whatever extra faith and hope they might be said to have, they are certainly lacking somewhat in charity.) Yet the imaginative vistas they lead us to are no less turned toward the past as than the bucolic daydreams ascribed to the "other" left; it is, after all, a matter of "recovering the dreams which transfixed many from the middle of the Nineteenth Century until the dawn of the neoliberal era" (Ibid.). In other words, it is a matter of bringing to its completion the eighteenth-century project of the metaphysical bootstrapping of Man by means of the nineteenth-century project of absolute technical mastery over the world; that is, of making good on the promises of the century of Reason by fulfilling the promises of the century of Progress. History repeats itself – by leapfrogging, as we can see.[23]

§ The "Accelerationist Manifesto" closes on a grave note: "The choice facing us is severe: either a globalized post-capitalism or a slow fragmentation towards primitivism, perpetual crisis, and planetary ecological collapse." The introduction of the perspective of "ecological collapse," or at least a *reference* to it, in the accelerationists' speculative horizon is no doubt a novelty and something to be welcomed (Wark 2013); but it seems equally evident that it signals a crisis in accelerationist theories of crisis. It makes the affirmation of "Promethean mastery" sound hollow, like a cry of encouragement to the besieged troops of the Moderns, a flag waved to boost the morale of combatants now that "first nature" has treacherously turned against the radiant self-propelled progression of "second nature," and the temporality of ecological crisis has started to resonate catastrophically with the temporality of economic crisis. The motif of acceleration thus acquires an entirely unexpected sense; for now it is no longer, or no longer only, a matter of the liberating acceleration of *productive forces*, but of the growing momentum of the *destructive forces* unleashed by the physical interaction between the capitalist system and the Earth System. For that reason, "planetary ecological collapse" can hardly be designated by the adjective "slow" (as in "a slow fragmentation toward primitivism" and so on). As we have seen, that collapse does not fully pertain to the realm of our "choice"; it is not only *ahead of* us, as the authors of the "Manifesto" appear to believe, it is to a good extent *behind* us: it has already started to happen and cannot be reverted, but only have its own acceleration *slowed down*. Capitalism's infra-economic substrate – the *material* conditions of current "material conditions" – is changing faster than the technical and political superstructures of the dominant civilization. There is no dialectic that can break this deadlock. The "intentional" acceleration of capitalist machinery, posed as a solution to our present anthropological destitution, finds itself in an objective contradiction with another, absolutely *not* intentional acceleration: the inexorable process of positive feedback of environmental transformations that have nefarious consequences for the species' *Umwelt*. There are strong reasons, in short, to fear that a globally integrated post-capitalism will not arrive fast enough to prevent a "slow" planetary ecological collapse. Paul Virilio's old dromology has been surpassed by a speed that is wholly *other*.

Noys (2014) observes that the agenda advanced in the "Accelerationist Manifesto" is not exactly original. Apart from regurgitating some points of Marx and Engel's hoary 1848 *Manifesto*, it repeats much of Gramsci's platform – with the disadvantage, as Noys points out, of failing to present any *concrete* strategy to dialectically control the *abstraction* that it at once denounces and praises. It seems to us, however, that the accelerationist program offers more than merely a techno upgrade of the Marxist vulgate. It is a strong version, in the sense of Lévi-Strauss's structural mythology, of what Oswald de Andrade (1990), in the (rejected) academic thesis that he wrote in 1950, called "messianic philosophy": the bimillenial patriarchal, repressive, transcendent, racist, and phallocratic narrative that runs like a red thread throughout the West's history, from Saint Paul to Marx, Husserl, Heidegger, and beyond. And here, much more than the youthful Williams and Srnicek, it is an old pontiff of the Universal who expresses to perfection what really moves accelerationists and explains their hostility to what they call "primitivism."

> I am not afraid of saying it [*de l'affirmer*]: ecology is the new opium of the masses. And as always, this opium has its official philosopher, which is [Peter] Sloterdijk. Being an affirmationist also means bypassing the intimidatory maneuvers made in the name of "nature." One must state [*affirmer*] clearly that humankind is an animal species that tries to surpass its animality, a natural ensemble that tries to denaturalize itself. (Badiou 2009)

It is hard to be clearer, more "affirmative" – three times in almost as many lines, in fact – and more off the mark. What Badiou calls "ecology," and which is actually the name of a *loss of faith* in the species' manifest destiny and in the earthly delights of communist sublimation, is demonized by him as a reactionary, superstitious movement that spreads a religion of fear – Alain Badiou, Luc Ferry, and Pascal Bruckner, *même combat?* – with the supreme gall of wishing to define the content of politics and the form of the political.[24] What tree huggers really want, then – though they shall not prevail – is to drag us back to the primal terrors of an animalized humankind, helpless in the face of an omnipotent and unpredictable Nature. The convergence between the discourse of accelerationists (and their gurus) with Singularitarianism and the vibrant capitalist apologetics of think tanks like the Breakthrough Institute, we are not afraid of stating it, is deeply disturbing.

Accelerationists believe that "we" must choose between the animal that we were and the machine that we shall be. In their materialist angelology, what they propose is, in short, a world without us – but made by us. Reciprocally, they imagine a post-human species re-created by a hyper-capitalist "material platform" – but without capitalists. A nature denatured by un-man. A materialism, at long last(!), spiritualized.[25]

The Great Indoors: Tarde's speculative speleology

We shall bring this section on contemporary anthropological futurology to a close by referring to a text from the past that we nonetheless find quite relevant to our present time. By virtue of its delirious conceptual invention and its subtle combination of lyricism and sarcasm, Gabriel Tarde's essay in philosophiction, *Fragment d'Histoire Future*, translated into English as *Underground Man*, offers one of the most interesting versions of the loss-of-the-world theme. Its virtue to our survey lies in taking the technophile progressivism characteristic of the Singularitarian and accelerationist variants outlined above to its own absurd limit, all the while making us reflect directly about our relationship to the Earth.

The *Fragment* is one of Tarde's first writings, in which he sketches out some ideas that will be key to his subsequent oeuvre. It is an imaginative exercise that intends, or rather pretends to intend – for the text superposes several layers of irony – to present the quintessence of society. It describes the emergence of a "wholly human humankind" [*une humanité toute humaine*] that results from an unexpected cosmic accident which had brought about the "complete elimination of living nature, whether animal or vegetable, man only excepted" (Tarde 1974: 111). The *Fragment*'s narrator is a historian who describes the past and the present of a Great Transformation that will have taken place in our future, a monumental anthropological *katabasis*: the descent of humankind (white and European, we are led to suppose) into the heart of the planet in response to a climate catastrophe.[26] After a long era of tedious prosperity, similar in nature to the one prophesized by the Breakthrough Institute – the end of wars, the consolidation of a "perfectly humdrum, regular, neuter, and even emasculated" [*si parfaitement bourgeois, correct, neutre et châtré*] (Ibid.: 48) world government, an economy based on an inexhaustible energetic matrix (sun, rivers, winds, tides), a single language – the "fortunate disaster" (Ibid.: 21) supervenes. The sun starts suffering from "aenemia" (Ibid.: 50), goes into collapse, dies out; the planet's surface freezes over, millions perish, and civilization is obliged to remodel itself from top to bottom "for the benefit of mankind" (Ibid.: 21).

The disaster is announced, but the reaction is late in coming: "the public concerned itself little about the matter, as in all that is gradual and not sudden" (Ibid.: 50). Until one spring day a somber reddish sun announces the final twilight: "the meadows were no longer green, the sky was no longer blue, the Chinese were no longer yellow" (Ibid.: 53). But far from developing into an interplanetary adventure of colonization of the Great Outdoors, the narrative, proceeding *ab exterioribus ad interiora* (Ibid.: 76), descends into a delirious speleological speculation.[27] Miltiades, humankind's saving genius, convinces the latter to burrow deep into the Earth, leaving behind the dying sun and investing in the overabundant energy furnished by the globe's igneous heart: "Let us descend into these depths; let us make these abysses our sure retreat" (Ibid.). The descent into a cave environment is depicted as a "complete restoration of the exiled soul to the land of its birth!" (Ibid.: 77), making Miltiades into an anti-Platonic sage or an antipodal Platonist, and the *Fragment* into an inverted allegory of the cave.[28] By virtue of a powerfully, prophetically Latourian rhetoric, this messiah of transdescendence captures his audiences' imagination and adhesion: "It is no more by this gesture (*the speaker raises his finger to heaven*) that the hope of salvation should henceforth be expressed, it is by this one. (*He lowers his right hand towards the earth.*)...We must say no more: 'Up there!', but 'below!' " (Ibid.: 75–6; italics in the original).[29]

Contrary to the Edenic scheme of the wilderness, the opposition between life and humanity mobilized by the *Fragment* places humanity and the inorganic world on the positive side of the equation, whereas non-human life is placed on the negative, "anti-social" side. The truth of man is his social, autopoietic dimension, not his organic, allopoietic one; and sociality is effectively affirmed as the background of the great Nature, the universal ontological condition. Psychology and chemistry, supreme sciences of association, fuse into a single sociomonadological knowledge: while chemists "construct for us the psychology of the atom, our psychologists explain to us the atomic theory of self, I was going to say the sociology of self" (Ibid.: 169). Man will reflect himself on rocks, metals, and atoms rather than a long-extinct fauna and flora, thus partaking in an elemental non-organic vitality that will finally free him from the idea of death, this biocentric phantasm.

This great inward migration, in search of the "*espace du dedans*" [space within], to evoke Henri Michaux, will take place in frontal contradiction to the biblical tale of Noah. This time, no other living being will be carried with us; Nature, this "miscellany of living contradictions" (Ibid.: 86), will be left behind, turned into mere frozen protein – the millions of animal carcasses stuck in the ice sheets on the surface will provide humankind with sustenance for centuries, until chemistry manages to make food out of rocks. Only the treasures of culture and technique will follow us down into the inside, in the shape of a gigantic library and a vast museum that will enable the flourishing of a new civilization, one that is refined, *purified*.[30] Post-catastrophic troglodytism is therefore not a regression toward a natural primitiveness, but, on the contrary, a supremely emancipatory artificialization, a physical interiorization *into* the world that is also a technical internalization *of* the world. Nature, no longer experienced as an obstacle to human freedom, is completely aestheticized and becomes a *myth*, taking on "the profound and intimate charm of an old legend, but it is a legend in which one believes" (Ibid.: 180).

The *Fragment* is rich in sociological provocations, caustic in its sarcasm against the socialist cult of work (Ibid.: 122ff), and thought-provoking in its association between a state of total aestheticization of life and full realization of Love as the founding sociocosmical bond (echoes of Fourier, perhaps?). Unlike the empire of lack and want, the well-known Hobbesian image of a solitary, poor, nasty, brutish, etc. life evoked in dystopias such as *Mad Max* and *The Road*, in Tarde's abiotic world needs have largely been met, and so become invisible: humankind is "obliged to," and manages to, extract everything "from its own resources, if not its food supplies" (Ibid.: 112).[31] The artistically superfluous has the upper hand over economistic utilitarianism, and the loving "exchange of reflections" can finally blossom without the instrumentalist illusion of the "exchange of services" (Ibid.: 116).

As we see it, however, the book's key is to be found in its final pages, which function as a sort of anti-magic cave (see von Trier's *Melancholia*) in what ultimately is, when all is said and done, a rather melancholy fantasy: the somewhat macabre enthusiasm of the historian of post-apocalyptic civilization gives way to a growing disquiet in the face of a focus of rebellion, an irreducible anti-social impulse of humankind. This technicized counter-Eden fails to liberate us from all atavisms. The perfect, but "excessive and compulsory" [*à outrance et forcée*] society of the future is not without its "malcontents" (Ibid.: 186–7), in whom the monotonous homogeneity of the artificial environment inspires nothing but ennui (accelerationism is not to everyone's taste…).[32] Even worse, this society finds itself threatened by the irruption of the most natural of instincts: spring rut not only stirs suicidal impulses of "transascendence" toward the planet's icy surface; it leads, in association with the material affluence of the new humankind, to a progressive and generalized relaxation of customs: to Malthusian disaster, that is, a demographic explosion.[33] In short, even the end of History must come to an end in time.[34]

6

A world of people

When the sky was still too close to Earth, there was nothing in the world except people and tortoises.

Aikewara myth

We find in the *Fragment* an important exception to the extinction of every other form of life apart from the narrator's civilization: the "little tribe of burrowing Chinese" (Tarde 1974: 157) discovered in one of the many internal explorations carried out by the new Terrans.[1] These Chinese, who had gone into the Earth unnoticed via the antipodes, had managed to bring to the depths a sort of miniature nature, and "raised underground diminutive vegetables in diminutive beds of soil they had brought thither together with diminutive pigs and dogs. . ." (Ibid.: 158). Giving up on either exterminating or subjugating that tribe of "degraded beings," who in fact had "shamelessly given themselves up to ancestral cannibalism," Miltiades' followers eventually decide to close again the dividing wall between the new subterranean civilization and this "veritable underground America" so "disgusting to our new Christopher Columbus" (Ibid.: 157–8). The cannibal Chinese are thus directly associated by Tarde with the indigenous inhabitants of the Americas, a continent around which, as Antonello Gerbi (2010) has shown in a classic study, a long historico-philosophical polemic took place about its stunted nature and the no less abortive humankind (notoriously given to cannibalism, as a matter of fact) to which it was home. Let us see then how the inhabitants of the real America formulated the problem of the relation between humanity, world, and history. It is these Amerindian mythocosmologies that bring to a close our attempt to survey, in no doubt too schematic a way, the various imaginaries of the end of the world that populate our world, who knows for how long.

The end of transformations, or the first Anthropocene

We have seen examples of mythical images of a literally pre-historical world, fully alive but still without humans, at the very least a world pre-dating the separation between man and world – the narrative about Eden and the Fall. We have seen its symmetrical image in Weisman's ecological *apokatastasis*, the disappearance of the human as a restitution of the world to itself. We then went through visions of a future in which everything will become "human," either because the world will have been diminished or annihilated by an environmental collapse (resulting in humans becoming monstrous predators of their own species, as in *The Road*, or hypnotized prey that provide the last source of living energy for the new mechanocosmic order, as in *The Matrix*); or because the world will have been transubstantiated and absorbed by humankind as the triumphant species that re-transcends itself, through ingenious feats of anthropo-engineering, into a sublime post-human entity capable of facing up to the challenge of a future of "abstraction, complexity, globality and technology" (Williams and Srnicek 2013). (This, as we have seen, also comes in two versions: capitalist governance or Soviets + cyborgs.) We have also followed a few inverted images, created by the subtraction of the "subject" pole in the humanity/world opposition: thus the idea of a world in which nothing is essentially living, let alone human, as in the hypothesis of a remote or "fossil," abiotic and extra-experiential past; or in the line of reasoning that leads to a radical devaluation of the present in favor of a future of cosmic extinction as the truth and destiny of Being (death as ontological argument).

We have noticed, besides, the central ambiguity that is a mark of the properly modern metaphysical condition, namely the "correlationist" figure of a transcendental or constitutive anteriority of the human vis-à-vis a world that nonetheless has empirical precedence over it, and the important consequence, among others, that this situation entails from the civilizational point of view: the manifest necessity of a re-determination of the empirical world – also, and perhaps above all, of the empirical human – by the human as transcendental negativity, through the thaumaturgic potency of labor and the emancipatory violence of revolution (thus the Promethean mastery of the "Accelerationist Manifesto" and the self-denaturing, biophobic vocation of Badiousian man).

There is, however, one other possible mythocosmological variant left: that in which the world is subtracted from the correlation with the human at the *beginning* rather than the end of times; a variant, in short, in which the human is placed as *empirically anterior* in relation to the world.

This is a hypothesis that is explored in several Amerindian cosmogonies. It finds itself conveniently summarized in the commentary that opens a myth of the Yawanawa, a people of Pano-speakers from the western Amazon: "The myth's action takes place in a time when 'nothing yet was, but people already existed'" (Carid 1999: 166; cited in Calavia 2001). The version of the Aikewara, a Tupian-speaking people who live on the other end of Amazonia, adds that curious exception: there was nothing in the world except people – and tortoises (Calheiros 2014: 41).

At first, then – originally – everything was human or, rather, nothing was not-human.[2] (Except for tortoises, of course, if we are to believe the Aikewara.) A considerable number of Amerindian myths – as well as, less usually perhaps, those from other ethnographic regions – imagine the existence of a primordial humanity, either fabricated by a demiurge or simply presupposed as the only substance or matter out of which the world would come to be formed. These are narratives about a time before the beginning of time, an era or aeon that we could call "pre-cosmological" (Viveiros de Castro 2007). These "primordial people" were not fully human in our sense, since, despite being anthropomorphic and endowed with the same mental faculties as we are, they possessed great anatomic plasticity and a certain penchant for immoral conducts (incest, cannibalism). After a series of exploits, parts of this primordial humankind progressively changed, either spontaneously or, again, under the action of a demiurge, into the biological species, geographical features, meteorological phenomena, and celestial bodies that compose the present cosmos. The part that did not change, remaining essentially equal to itself, is the historical, or contemporary, humankind.[3]

One of the best illustrations, if not the best, of this general type of cosmology is exposed in great detail and with admirable elegance in the autobiography of Yanomami shaman and political leader Davi Kopenawa (Kopenawa and Albert 2013; see also Albert 1985). More succinctly, we could also recall ideas from the Ashaninka (Campa), an Arawak people both geographically and culturally distant from the Yanomami:

> Campa mythology is largely the story of how, one by one, the primal Campa became irreversibly transformed into the first representatives of various species of animals and plants, as well as astronomical bodies or features of the terrain...The development of the universe, then, has been primarily a process of diversification, with mankind as the primal substance out of which many if not all of the categories of beings and things in the universe arose, the Campa of today being the descendants of those ancestral Campa who escaped being transformed. (Weiss 1972: 169–70)[4]

We could also mention the cosmogony of the Luiseño from California, evoked by Lévi-Strauss (1988: 141–55) in *The Jealous Potter*, in which the cultural hero Wyiot differentiates the originary human community into the various species of currently existing beings. The theme is also found in some non-Amerindian cultures: for example, the Kaluli from Papua New Guinea recount that "at that [pre-cosmological] time, according to the prevailing story, there were no trees or animals or streams or sago or food. The earth was covered entirely with people" (Schieffelin 1976: 94). A man of prestige and authority (a *big man*, in Melanesian parlance) then decided to transform the different groups of people into different species and other natural phenomena: "those who were left aside became the ancestors of human beings."

We thus see how, in Amerindian thought, humanity or personhood is both the seed and the primordial ground, or background, of the world.[5] *Homo sapiens* is not the character who comes to crown the Great Chain of Being by adding a new ontological layer (spiritual or "cognitive," in modern parlance) on top of a previously existing organic layer that would, in turn, have emerged out of a substrate of "dead" matter. In the West's mythophilosophical tradition, we tend to conceive animality and "nature" in general as referring essentially to the past. Animals are living "archefossils," not only because beasts roamed the Earth long before we did (and because these archaic beasts were like magnified versions of present animals), but because "anatomically modern humans" have their origin in prior species that are closer to pure animality the more we recede in time.[6] By virtue of a felicitous innovation – bipedalism, neoteny, cooperation, syntactical language, etc. – the Great Watchmaker, whether blindly or omnividently, conferred upon us a capacity that made us into more-than-organic beings (in the sense of Alfred Kroeber's "superorganic"), endowed with that spiritual supplement that is "proper to man": the species' precious *private property*. Human exceptionalism, in short: language, labor, law, desire; time, world, death. Culture. History. Future. Humans belong to the future just as animals belong to the past – our past, since animals themselves are, or so we would like to think, trapped inside an exiguous world within an immobile present.

§ The exception here once again comes from works of fiction, such as the *Planet of the Apes* series produced by Arthur Jacobs, in which human civilization gives way to an ape civilization which nonetheless repeats the same vices and "sins" of their erstwhile masters: a militarized, totalitarian society that enslaves, humiliates and tortures its others, humans now deprived of voice and language (or simply mute), going so far as using them as laboratory rats in scientific research. The first two films of the series, *The Planet of the Apes* (1968) and *Beneath the Planet of the Apes* (1970), situate the narrative in a dystopian future (dystopian for humans, that is); *Escape from the Planet of the Apes* (1971), *Conquest of the Planet of the Apes* (1972), as well as the recent reboot *The Rise of the Planet of the Apes* (2011), tell the story of how the apes' revolt and escape, which would eventually lead to the reversal of roles between them and humans, came about. In the latter film, the contingent event that would at once explain that reversal and the apes' successful escape is the unexpected side effect of an experimental drug injected into the ape protagonist, Caesar, in the context of an Alzheimer's disease research: the development of its intelligence, which eventually leads to the acquisition of language. The animal at the end of the human's future is thus a hybrid, a genetically modified organism that takes revenge on its creator. This cannot but bring to mind Ridley Scott's *Blade Runner* (1982), based on Philip K. Dick's *Do Androids Dream of Electric Sheep?*, whose non-human protagonists are not animals (there are no longer any animals in that dystopian future, except as artificial replica), but humanoid machines.

Yet that is not, as we can see, how things go as far as these *other humans* that are the Amerindians and other non-modern collectives are concerned. One of the things that make them "other" consists precisely in the fact that their concepts of "human" (and of "world") are other to our own. The world as we know it, or rather the world as the indigenous knew it, the "present" world that exists (or existed) in the interval between the time of origins and the end of times – the intercalary time that we could call "ethnographic present" or the present of ethnos, as opposed to the "historical present" of the nation-state – this world is conceived in some Amerindian cosmologies as the epoch that began when pre-cosmological beings suspended their ceaseless becoming-other (erratic metamorphoses, anatomic plasticity, "unorganized" corporeality) in favor of greater ontological univocality.[7] Putting an end to the "time of transformations" – a common expression among Amazonian cultures – those unstable primordial anthropomorphs took on the forms and bodily dispositions of those animals, plants, rivers, mountains, etc. that they would come to be. This was, in fact, already prefigured in the names that they bore in that absolute past; thus, for example, the "Peccary Yanomami" – the tribe of originary people who had the name "Peccary" – "became peccaries," that is, the wild pigs that the Yanomami hunt and eat today. (*Yanomami* means "people" or "proper human being" in the language of the Yanomami, as opposed to *napë*, which means Other or enemy.) The "whole world" – though again perhaps not the tortoises or some other oddity – is virtually included in this originary proto-humankind. The pre-cosmological situation might thus be indifferently described as a still worldless humanity or as a world in human form, an anthropomorphic multiverse that eventually gave way to a world conceived as the result of the (never quite finished) stabilization of the infinite potential for transformability contained in humanity as universal "substance," or rather universal "actance," both originary and persistent.[8]

We can thus find here a multiple inversion of the cannibalistic or zombie apocalypse scenarios that figure in Cormac McCarthy's *The Road* and similar narratives: in indigenous mythology, human food consists of humans that morphed into animals and plants; humanity is the active principle at the origin of the proliferation of living forms in a rich, plural world. But the indigenous scheme is also an inversion of the Garden of Eden myth: in the Amerindian case, humans are the first to come, and the rest of creation proceeds from them. It is as if what comes from Adam's rib is much more than his female complement – the whole world, the entire infinite rest of it. And names, in their infinite variety, existed, as we have seen, before-alongside things (the Peccary Yanonami, the nation of Jaguars, the Canoes-in-human-form, etc.); things did not wait for a human arche-namer to get to know *that* they were, and *what* they were. Everything was *human*, but everything was not *one*. Humankind was a polynomic multitude; it appeared from the start in the form of an internal multiplicity whose morphological externalization – that is, speciation – is precisely the stuff of cosmogonic narrative. It is Nature that is *born* out of or "separates" itself from Culture, not the other way round, as in our anthropophilosophical vulgate.

We can therefore see that the subsumption of the world by humankind in Amerindian cosmologies travels in a direction opposite to that of the myth of technological Singularity. It refers to the past, not the future; its emphasis is on the stabilization of the transformations that came to differentiate animals from those humans who continued to be so, not on accelerating the transformation of the animals that we "were" into the machines we "will be." Indigenous praxis lays stress on the regulated production of transformations that are capable of reproducing the ethnographic present (life-cycle rituals, the metaphysical management of death, shamanism as cosmic diplomacy), and thus to thwart the regressive proliferation of chaotic transformations. Control is required because the world's transformative potential, as attested by the omnipresent traces of the action of a universal anthropomorphic intentionality, manifests a remanence that is at once *dangerous* and *necessary*. *Danger* lies in the fact that former humans retain a human virtuality underneath their present animal, vegetal, astral, artifactual, etc. appearance, in a similar (but symmetrically opposed) way to how we often fantasize about being wild animals deep down under our civilized guise. Non-humans' archaic humanoid latency – humanity as the animal's unconscious, we could say – constantly threatens to break through the tears that open up in the fabric of the everyday world (dreams, illnesses, hunting incidents), violently reabsorbing humans back into the pre-cosmological substrate where all differences continue to chaotically communicate with each other.[9] In turn, the *necessity* of this remanence lies in the fact that the actualization of the ethnographic present presupposes a recapitulation or counter-effectuation of the pre-cosmological state, as that is the reservoir of all difference, all dynamism, and therefore all possibility of sense. The anthropomorphic multiverse, in its originary virtuality, is thus both conjured through and kept at bay by an animalization of the human – the theriomorphic mask of the spirit-dancer, the becoming-beast of the warrior – which is reciprocally a mythical humanization of the animal (Viveiros de Castro 1998). It is from this double movement that *ethnos* ceaselessly emerges. The ethnographic present is in no way an immobile "time"; slow societies know infinite speeds, extra-historical accelerations – in short, *becomings* – that make the indigenous concepts of *buen vivir* ("good living") something metaphysically much closer to a radical sport than to a peaceful retirement in the countryside.

What we could call "natural world," or "world" for short, is for Amazonian peoples a multiplicity of intricately connected multiplicities. Animal and other species are conceived as so many kinds of "people" or "societies," that is, as *political entities*. It is not "the jaguar" that is "human";

it is individual jaguars that take on a subjective dimension (more or less relevant according to the practical context of interaction with them) when they are perceived as having "behind" them a society, a collective political alterity.[10] To be sure, we too – by which is meant us Westerners, a concept that includes, through mere convention, Brazilians of European descent – think, or would like to think that we think, that it is only possible to be human in society, that man is a political animal, etc. But Amerindians think that there are many more societies (and therefore also humans) between heaven and earth than are dreamt of in our philosophy and anthropology. What we call "environment" is for them a society of societies, an international arena, a *cosmopoliteia*. There is, therefore, no absolute difference in status between society and environment, as if the first were the "subject," the second the "object." Every object is another subject, and is more than *one*. The watchword that every novice left-wing militant learns, according to which "everything is political," acquires in the Amerindian case a radical literality – including the indeterminacy of this "everything"; see our famous tortoises...– that not even the most enthusiastic activist in the streets of Copenhagen, Rio, or Madrid might be ready to admit.

Anthropomorphism *contra* anthropocentrism

If the Amerindian concept of "nature," once we take the term as designating the sphere of non-human existents, is distinct from ours – since non-humans are seen as ex-humans that preserve a latent or secret human side which remains imperceptible to us under normal conditions – their concept of humanity or "culture" will perforce be no less so. Amerindians are part of that enormous minority of peoples who have never been modern, as they have never had a Nature that they either have lost or needed to liberate themselves from. It should be noted that, between their humanity and ours, as well as between their world and ours, it is not simply a matter of differing cultural visions of a same natural world (the world as described more or less exhaustively by modern sciences); nor of different cultural worlds imagined by a same

humankind considered as a natural species. Both sides of the
anthropocosmological equation must be modified simultaneously, which results in a displacement of the problem; not
because the two variables of the equation are in "correlation"
with each other, but because the very correlation as we tend
to imagine it – be it in order to affirm it or to deny it – ceases
to make sense when we translate it into Amerindian terms.

We are of course speaking of so-called "Amerindian perspectivism," of which we fear it might be inevitable to say
a couple of words, even at risk of making those who have
heard more than enough about the subject flee. "Amerindian
perspectivism" was thus the name chosen by Tânia Stolze
Lima (1996, 2005) and Eduardo Viveiros de Castro (1998,
2014) to designate a broadly shared notion in indigenous
America, according to which each existing species sees itself
as (anatomically and culturally) human, since what it sees
of itself is its "soul," that is, an internal image that is like
a shadow or echo of the ancestral humanoid background
common to all beings. The soul, always anthropomorphic,
is the aspect that existing beings see of themselves and of
others when they look at and interact with beings of the
same species – this is, in fact, what defines the idea of "same
species." The external corporeal form of a species is therefore the way in which it is seen by *other* species (this form is
often described as a "clothing"). Thus, when a jaguar looks
at another jaguar, it sees a man (an Indian): a fellow human
citizen, although, significantly, one that is decorated with
the distinctive ornaments of the Jaguar People (jaguar tooth
necklaces, spotted body painting...). But when it looks at
a man – what Indians see as a man – it sees a peccary or
a monkey, as these are among the Amazonian indigenous'
favorite game. Every existing being in the cosmos thus sees
itself as human, but does not see other species in the same
way. (Needless to say, this also applies to our own species.)
"Humanity" is therefore at once a universal condition and a
strictly deictic, self-referential perspective. Different species
cannot occupy the point of view of "I" simultaneously, owing
to deictic restriction; in every confrontation here and now
between two species, it is inevitable that one will finish by
imposing its humanity on the other, that is, that it will finish
by making the other "forget" its own humanity.[11]

This entails that we humans (Amerindian humans, that is) do not see animals as humans. They are not human *for us*; but we know they are human *for themselves*.[12] We know just as well that we are not human *for them*: that they see us as game, or ferocious predators, or powerful enemy tribes (whose merely taxonomic "humanity" is irrelevant, if not actively denied), or cannibal spirits, depending on our respective positions in the food chain. When an Indian interacts with a being from "another species" – which includes, we stress again, the members of other collectives that *we* would call "human" – he or she knows that they are dealing with an entity that is human in its own domain. It thus follows that every trans-specific interaction in Amerindian worlds is an international intrigue, a diplomatic negotiation, or a war operation that must be undertaken with maximum circumspection: cosmopolitics.

Like all human beings – or more precisely: like all animals – Amerindians must eat or in some way destroy other forms of life in order to live. They know that human action inevitably leaves an "ecological footprint" on the world. Differently to us, however, the ground on which they leave their footprints is *equally* alive and alert, often being the zealously guarded domain of some super-subject (the master-spirit of the forest, for example). One must always be very careful where one steps. As Leibniz, the patron saint of philosophical perspectivism, used to say, "there are souls everywhere." In short, the fundamental postulate of Amerindian cosmopolitics is what is commonly called *anthropomorphism*, a concept that we do not think should be used pejoratively, as it so often is when condescendingly applied to "primitive" people and other such "simple" souls. On the contrary: aside from the fact that this pragmatico-ontological presupposition is largely disseminated in the eponymous species (we know the troubles that modern science had to go through in order to restrict its validity to specific domains), we are of the opinion that anthropomorphism should be granted full philosophical citizenship owing to the as yet unexplored conceptual possibilities it opens.

We shall therefore define the "animist" outlook of Amerindians and similar peoples as *ontologies* (or perhaps counterontologies) manifesting the anthropomorphic principle, so as to contrast them from the anthropocentric principle that strikes us as constituting one of the most solid pillars of Western metaphysics, in its "dogmatic" or "speculative" variants as well as, of course, in critical philosophy and other "correlationist" drifts.[13] In this sense, anthropomorphism is a perfectly ironic (dialectical?) inversion of anthropocentrism. To say that everything is human is to say that humans are not a special species, an exceptional event that came to tragically or magnificently interrupt the monotonous trajectory of matter in the universe. Anthropocentrism, conversely, makes humans into an animal species endowed with a transfiguring supplement; it takes them for beings traversed by transcendence as if by a supernatural arrow, stamped with a stigma, an opening, or a privileged lack (*felix culpa*) that indelibly marks them out in the middle – at the center – of Nature. And when Western philosophy penitentially undergoes self-critique and tries to attack anthropocentrism, its way of negating human exceptionalism consists in affirming that we are, at a fundamental level, animals, or living beings, or material systems *like all the rest*; "materialist" reduction or elimination is the favored method for bringing humans down to the same level as the pre-existing world. The anthropomorphic principle, in contrast, states that animals and other beings are human *just like us* ("somewhat like us" would be more accurate): "pan-psychic" generalization or expansion is the basic method for bringing the world up to the same level as the ancestral pan-humanoid condition.

It could be objected that, rigorously speaking, animals are humans-for-themselves *for us*, since it is "we" (the Amerindians) who *know* this and act accordingly. No doubt. But we do not know all that the animals know, let alone all that they are.[14] At any rate, this does not mean that there is, somewhere in the world's hidden depths, a Human-in-itself or an Animal-in-itself, since there is no distinction in Amerindian metaphysics (and here we advance an ethnographic thesis, not a universalist hypothesis) between the "world-in-itself" and the indeterminate series of existing beings understood as centers of perspectives or, if one prefers, as monads. Each object or aspect of the universe is a hybrid entity, at once human-for-itself and not-human-for-an-other, or rather, by-an-other. In this sense, every existing being, and the world as open aggregate of existing beings, is a *being-outside-of-itself*. There is no being-in-itself, being-qua-being, that does not depend on its being-as-other; every being is being-by, being-for, being-relation (Latour 2013d).[15] Exteriority is everywhere. The Great Outdoors, like charity, starts at home.

Inverting Brassier's formula (and emphasis), the Amerindian philosopher should therefore conclude: "everything is always already *alive*."[16] Which does not prevent (much on the contrary) death from being a fundamental motif and motor of life, human life in particular.[17] And from *this* point of view, Indians curiously do agree with speculative nihilism and the need to step out of the narcissistic circle of correlation:

> Whites only treat us as ignorant because we are different from them. But their thought is short and obscure; it cannot go far and elevate itself, *because they want to ignore death*. (...) Whites do not dream far like we do. *They sleep a lot, but they only dream about themselves.* (Kopenawa and Albert 2013: 411–12; our emphasis)

Kopenawa connects the vain desire to ignore death with the Whites' obsession with the property relation and the commodity-form. They are "*in love*" with commodities, in which their thought remains "*trapped*": "Thus, they *dream* about their cars, their houses, their money and all their other goods... " (Kopenawa and Albert 2013: 437–9; our emphasis). Let us remember that the Yanomami not only ascribe the highest value to prodigality and non-mercantile exchange, they also destroy all the possessions of their dead.[18]

"*Whites sleep a lot, but they only dream about themselves.*" This is perhaps the cruelest judgment ever passed on the anthropological characteristic of the "Whites" – those that Latour would call "Moderns" or, more perversely, "Humans." Whites' epistemic devaluation of dreams would thus go hand in hand with their solipsistic fascination with themselves – their incapacity to discern the secret humanity of non-human beings – and their "fetishistic" avarice, as ridiculous as it is incurable. Whites, in short, dream with what *has no sense*.[19]

It is interesting to notice that, on the one hand, there is something profoundly pertinent from the psychoanalytic point of view in Kopenawa's diagnosis – his *Traumdeutung* of the Whites would put many a Freudo-Marxist thinker to shame – and, on the other, this diagnosis pays us back with our own false coin. After all, the accusation of a narcissistic projection of the Ego onto the world is something that the Moderns have always resorted to in order to define the anthropological characteristic of "animist" peoples – Freud himself being, as is well known, one of the most illustrious advocates of this thesis.[20] According to those we call animists, in contrast, it is we Moderns who, when we enter the space of exteriority and truth – that is, dreaming – can only see haunting reflections and simulacra of ourselves, rather than opening up to the disquieting strangeness of commerce with an infinity of agencies, at once intelligible and radically other, that proliferate across the cosmos. The Yanomami present us with the politics of dream against the state: not our "dream" of a society against the state, but dreams as a society against the state dreams them.

The end of the world of the Indians

The same shaman prophesized, in his indictment of the eco-suicidal vertigo of the civilization that creepingly suffocates the "forest-world"[21] of the Yanomami: "Whites are not afraid of being crushed by the falling sky as we are. But one day they will be, maybe as much as we are!" (Kopenawa and Albert 2013: 540). This day is apparently dawning. In an unusually "primitivist" passage of his treatise on the anthropology of the Moderns, Latour (2013d: 454–5) remarks that "the multiplicity of nonhumans that the ecological crises thrust together in all sectors of the Economy" troublingly poses once again the question, at once "economic" and "ethical," of the relationship between means and ends; and, lo and behold, we start to see among us, Latour concludes, a "gradual return to the ancient cosmologies and their anxieties, as we suddenly notice that they were not all that ill founded."[22]

The prophecy about the fall of the sky, expressed with extraordinary eloquence in Kopenawa's testimony, is a recurrent theme in various Amerindian eschatologies. More usually than not, these universal collapses, sometimes associated with layered cosmographies including several "skies" and "earths"

piled on top of one another, are periodical phenomena, a part
of large cycles of destruction and re-creation of humankind
and the world. It is common that such stratigraphic rear-
rangements be ascribed to the aging of the cosmos and the
growing weight of the dead (be it of their corpses under the
earth, be it of their souls on the celestial layer). This may
result, as is the case in Yanomami cosmology, in a cascading
fall of celestial layers, which come to occupy the place of
the former terrestrial layers, which in turn become subterranean worlds; their inhabitants (we, the living of today)
then become cannibal monsters of the infra-world, while the
celestial souls of the dead become the new humankind of the
new terrestrial layer. In other eschatologies, the destruction of
the world is due to very classic, but still efficacious (judging
from the present climate crisis) causes: universal cataclysm
(deluge) or conflagration (fire). In the case of the Guarani
of Southern Brazil and the Paraná-Paraguay Basin, successive Earths and their respective humankind have been (and
shall be) created and destroyed by the gods, by fire or by
water, or yet by the withdrawal of the structure that sustains
the terrestrial layer.[23] In the imminent next destruction, the
eschatology of the Guarani-Ñandeva, famously described by
Nimuendaju (1987), predicts that a giant blue jaguar shall
descend from the skies to devour humankind, while the pillars
of the Earth fall apart and everything is drawn into the eternal
abyss.[24]

What seems to be a constant in indigenous mythologies
concerning the end of the world is the unthinkability of a
world without people, without a humankind of some sort,
however different from ours – as a matter of fact, the humankinds of each cosmic era generally tend to be entirely alien
to each other, like separate species. The destruction of the
world is the destruction of humankind and vice versa; the
re-creation of the world is the re-creation of some form of
life, that is, of experience and perspective; and, as we have
seen, the *form* of every life is "human." The idea of a final
and definitive destruction of the world is equally rare, if at
all existent, among these cosmologies. Humankind is con-
substantial to the world or, rather, *objectively* "co-relational"
with the world, relational *as* the world. There is no "correlation" between epistemology and ontology, thought and

Being, but real immanence between existence and experience in the constitution of a relational multiverse.

This world that proceeds ontologically from humans (that is, from Indians) includes, we should note, Whites and their material civilization. These are generally conceived as descendants of a group of people who, in the beginning of time, were sent away from the center of the world by the demiurge because of their aggressive or greedy behavior, returning unexpectedly several centuries later.[25] Their arrival in the Americas was, and continues to be, the source of much metaphysical perplexity among indigenous peoples. This perplexity gave way (after five centuries of betrayals and genocides) to much indignation and apprehension, and tends to develop on the practico-speculative plane into a variety of counter-historical assemblages, such as prophetism, autonomist insurrection, the hope in cosmic renewal through catastrophe (the Quechua *pachakuti*, for example), the strategic reformulation of native shamanism in an ecopolitical language...In all these cases, what is at stake is affirming the ethnographic present, conserving or recovering it, not "growing," "progressing," or "evolving." As Andean peoples profess in their by now well-known cosmopolitical motto: *vivir bien, no mejor* (to live well, not better).

As we have seen, periodical apocalypses are the rule in Amerindian mythologies. When, however, these mythologies cross-pollinate with the mass of information that reaches indigenous peoples from all sides concerning the ongoing climate catastrophe; when this information adds up to the even more worrisome, because arising from direct experience, observation of a desynchronization of seasonal rhythms and hydrological cycles, and a consequent perturbation of the biosemiotic interactions characteristic of these peoples' traditional habitats;[26] when on top of that there is the generalized and mounting violent destruction of these environments by the programs for the acceleration of growth[27] pushed forward by nation-states in thrall to Integrated World Capitalism, not to speak of the already old penetration, much accelerated in recent times, of apocalyptic eschatologies disseminated among the indigenous by fundamentalist evangelical missionary sects – in these conditions, ever more present today in the indigenous Americas, the distress regarding the patent impossibility of reproducing the ethnographic present acquires a sense of urgency that is downright pessimistic.

The Yanomani, like other neighboring peoples (such as the Wajãpi), associate the weakening and decay of the terrestrial layer, as well as the emission of pathogenic outpourings that spread epidemics and cause the biological extinction of species, with mining activities (gold, cassiterite) taking place in their territories (Albert 1988, 1993; Kopenawa and Albert 2013; Gallois 1987). As they see it, the ignorance of the Whites (nicknamed "giant armadillos" or "monster peccaries" owing to their non-stop digging and upsetting the soil) regarding the agency of spirits and shamans that sustain the cosmological status quo has already started unleashing a supernatural revenge in the form of droughts and floods in various parts of the planet. Soon enough, with the death of the last Yanomami shamans, evil spirits will take over the cosmos, the sky will collapse, and we will all be annihilated. Kopenawa still admits that it is possible that, a long time from now, another humankind will come into being, but present "earth-eating Whites" will disappear alongside the indigenous (Kopenawa and Albert 2013: 540).

The Mbyá-Guarani, in turn, have recently developed an eschatology in which the re-creation of the world and humankind after the catastrophe will not include, as it did in the previous re-creation, the Whites (Pierri 2013, 2014b). Today's Earth will not exactly be destroyed, as it was the first time around; it will only undergo a spring cleaning: the thick layer of soil that covers the imperishable rock foundations of the terrestrial plateau will be scraped and thrown into the ocean by Nhanderu, the Mbyá's top deity; this will wipe away all the garbage, poison, and evil that Whites have left in their wake. The whole of humankind will perish in one purifying sweep. The Mbyá, however, will be re-created by Nhanderu to populate once again a renewed world; as for the Whites, they will vanish for good, and this time there will be no one left of this accursed species to start it all over again.[28] Among certain Guarani of Brazil's southeastern coast, a prophecy has been recorded involving the risk of accidents in the nuclear power plant situated in their territory. A shaman has evoked the cataclysm that destroyed the first humankind in order to predict an imminent second one: "The first [world] died by water, this one is marked to die by fire. (...) The White has studied, knows how to write, they already knew that this world would die by fire, so they said, 'let us build the Nuclear Plant straight away so that everything can be consumed by fire.' "[29]

The fact of the matter is that, for several Amerindian peoples, who never imagined the world would last forever, nor that their ethnographic present could effectively be eternal, let alone transform itself continuously into an ever more glorious future, the destruction of the present world is more and more seen as something imminent; it is indeed something that has already begun. Oiara Bonilla (personal communication, 2013) tells us of a conversation she had in November 2013 with a Guarani-Kaiowá healer from Mato Grosso do Sul. This state in the Brazilian Midwest, roughly equivalent in size to Poland, has been literally devastated by industrial agro-capitalism, more specifically in this case the monocultures of soya and sugarcane. The healer explained to Bonilla that various signs had already started to announce the coming end of the world. Apart from the violent storms that had castigated her village in the previous months, she recounted cockerels had begun to crow systematically out of time and – worst of all signs – she had overheard their chickens conversing "just like people." We know that when the world ends animals will once again be human as they were in mythical times; our dogs, chickens, wild beasts will all speak our language once more – until, we suppose, a new plane of immanence is traced, that is, a new "section of chaos" is selected (Deleuze and Guattari 1994: 42) and a new world can appear. Or, precisely, not.

Let us conclude by remarking that the apparent impossibility of conceiving of the end of the world as implying the definitive disappearance of every kind of humanity or of life – the impossibility of separating the idea of world from the idea of life, and this idea from that of agency, perspective or experience – is a simple transposition into the future of the fundamental notion of an anthropomorphic origin of all that exists. There may have been a humanity before the world; but there can be no world after humanity, that is, a world that lacks relation and otherness.

But that is not all. We shall see that Amerindians have something more to teach us about the end of the world.

7

Humans and Terrans
in the Gaia War

What do you do, after you stop pretending?
Dougald Hine,
The Dark Mountain Project

As we saw at the start of this book, there is a growing sentiment in contemporary culture – though by no means a unanimous, let alone consistent, conviction (Latour 2013b) – that
the two actants in our mytho-anthropology, "humankind"
and "world," (species and planet, societies and their environments, subject and object, thought and being, etc.) have
entered a nefarious cosmological or spatiotemporal conjunction associated with the controversial names of "Anthropocene" and "Gaia." The first name designates a new "time,"
or rather a new age of time – a new concept and a new
experience of temporality – in which the difference of magnitude between the scale of human history and the biological and geophysical scales has decreased dramatically, if not
reversed, with the environment changing faster than society.
With that, the near future becomes not only increasingly
unforeseeable, but perhaps also increasingly impossible. The
second name, "Gaia," designates a new way of experiencing
"space," drawing attention to the fact that our world, the
Earth, having suddenly become at once exiguous and fragile,
susceptible and implacable, has taken on the appearance of a
threatening Power that evokes those uncaring, unpredictable,

and unfathomable deities of our archaic past. Unpredictability, unfathomability, and a sense of panic in the face of a loss of control, if not of hope altogether: these are no doubt new challenges for modernity's proud intellectual assuredness.

Three authors have served us thus far as guides in our analysis, not only because they recognize the magnitude and gravity of current transformations, but because they insist on the need for a metaphysical reinvention – a reconceptualization and/or refiguration – of the notions of humanity and world elicited by the Anthropocene's and Gaia's bursting on the scene: Chakrabarty, Anders, and Latour.[1]

The impossible species

In "The Climate of History," Dipesh Chakrabarty drew attention to the fact that the Anthropocene seems to demand the recovery of the concept, refused outright by critical theories of capitalist globalization, of "humanity" as denoting the "human species." This is because, he claims, the consequences of climate catastrophe are only comprehensible when we think of humans as a form of life, and their more recent trajectory ("holocenic" in the strict etymological sense) as part of the long history of life on Earth. That does not mean, of course, that we should subscribe to pre-Darwinian speciesist essentialism, or some kind of sociotechnical teleologism, ignoring the historically contingent character of capitalism and its dependency on the intensive use of fossil fuels. However, we need an understanding of that which, outside the narrow limits of History as an academic discipline, pertains to so-called "deep history"[2] – the cultural-genetic mutations themselves brought about by oscillations and multicyclical or catastrophic changes in the behavior of the Earth System that created humankind hundreds of thousands of years ago – if we are to come to grips with how dependent we, as a species among others, are on other Earth species, and therefore on the planetary thermodynamic conditions which sustain the present biosphere and which are, as we know, to a large extent reciprocally conditioned by it. Global warming will bring changes that will remain for several tens of centuries, maybe even hundreds of thousands of years. Not even capitalism will last so long – which is at least some consolation, after all.

Whereas responsibility for environmental collapse cannot be uniformly distributed – it is glaringly obvious which geographical regions and social segments benefited historically from the processes that set it in motion – its consequences will be much more so: the Anthropocene, Chakrabarty (2009: 218) alerts us, "points to a shared catastrophe." In any case, we all know how the geopolitical landscape is changing in that respect, with the rise of China, India, Brazil, and so on as economic powerhouses with a promising ecotoxic future, and how this veritable arms race as regards the acceleration of growth has played a part in further complicating the diplomatic impasses around the environmental "question," already complicated in view of the inertia, intransigence, and greed of core capitalist countries.[3] Everything takes place as if some of the erstwhile victims wished to claim their own share in the now enviable condition (*cui bono?*) of future culprits of the shared catastrophe.

The polemical note in "The Climate of History" resides in the assertion that the history (historicity) of climate change does not fit within the history (and historiography) of globalization, which entails that the usual critique of capitalism runs the risk of tragically underestimating the real problem:

> The problematic of globalization allows us to read climate change only as a crisis of capitalist management. While there is no denying that climate change has profoundly to do with the history of capital, a critique that is only a critique of capital is not sufficient for addressing questions relating to human history once (...) the Anthropocene has begun to loom on the horizon of our present. (Chakrabarty 2009: 212).

It remains the case that the biocosmopolitical consciousness required by the new age would call for a kind of historical subject that Chakrabarty paradoxically regards as impossible: humankind as a species, precisely. According to him, the concept of species, politically mobilized by naturalists such as Edmund Wilson, plays "a quasi-Hegelian role (...) in the same way as the multitude or the masses in Marxist writings," but it is (as opposed to the Marxist masses?) a collective identity that is phenomenologically empty.[4] Human beings, says Chakrabarty, never *experience* themselves as a species; they can only *intellectually* apprehend themselves as a case of the concept:

> Even if we were to emotionally identify with a word like mankind, we would not know what being a species is, for, in species history, humans are only an instance of the concept species as indeed would be any other life form. But one never experiences being a concept. (Ibid.: 220).[5]

We admit to our difficulty in following the author's line of reasoning at this crucial juncture. It is possible that what Chakrabarty lacks here, so to speak, is greater attention to those subaltern peoples and discourses that he has analyzed so well elsewhere.[6] What is missing is perhaps a conceptual *analogon* that could play the role of that originary pre-specific and pre-historic, generic nature of the "humankind" that we encounter in indigenous mythologies; a genericity which, precisely, affords the humankind of reference[7] (the *ethnos* as "concrete universal") the possibility of a phenomenological apprehension, as intense as one may wish, of its own precarious specificity as affectual being, lived corporeality, perspectival subjectivity in perpetual cosmopolitical tension with the other humankinds hidden under the corporeality of other species. The ontological solidarity of the "human species" (i.e., the *ethnos* of reference) with the other peoples, collectives, and interests that populate, dispute, and constitute the Earth is not, for many non-modern people, the inert (conceptual) consequence of a natural history, but an active (experiential) given of the social history of the ensemble of the living as differentiated actualization of a pre-cosmological anthropomorphic potency. Chakrabarty's concept of the Anthropocene, in short, seems to us to require a little more ethnological comparativism and translative curiosity.[8]

This capital text – one of the great merits of which, to our minds, resides in the admission of the insufficiency of the critique of capitalism to account for planetary crisis – thus ends with a surprising confession of perplexity.[9] The human species, Chakrabarty concludes, can perhaps be the provisional name of the subject of a "new universal history of humans" (Ibid.: 221). But, he adds, "we can never understand this universal...that arises from a shared sense of a catastrophe" (Ibid.: 222) – from a shared sense of the imminence, that is, "of a naked apocalypse, an apocalypse without the Kingdom" (Anders 2007: 92), instead of the glorious transfiguration of the revolutionary apocalypse that prepares the Kingdom, in the Christian and Marxist style.[10] This is a universal that cannot positively subsume particulars, and which for that reason only deserves the name of "'a *negative human history*'" (Chakrabarty 2009: 221–2; our italics). Which would mean perhaps that humankind's only common finality is its end, its extinction? In fact, for as long as one tacks onto "universal history," taken as self-evident, the ambiguous restrictive qualification "human," it seems to us that it will be difficult to exit the Anthropocene both intellectually and "phenomenologically," and to pay all the necessary attention to the intrusion of Gaia.

Despite resorting to the notion of species (or "*genre*," at least in the French translation that we have referred to throughout this book) in his reflection on the mutation undergone by humankind with the advent of the nuclear age – namely, our passage from the condition of a "genre of mortals" to a "mortal genre," a species whose end has become metaphysically imminent – Günther Anders (2007) insists on the deceiving character of expressions such as "the threat of humankind to itself" or "atomic suicide." These evoke an image of humankind as an entity endowed with a single universal essence, but with a "soul" that is tragically torn between two possible actions, "pushing" or "not pushing" the button of nuclear holocaust, the struggle between which would thus take place inside each one of us, perhaps as a conflict between two opposed inclinations of our soul or generic essence.[11] This conception is attractive to the extent that it allows some room for hope, the hope that our will, this supposedly neutral instance, could exercise the role of judge, making the good choice provided it is informed by reason. Yet Anders thinks, much to the contrary, that we have no right to dissimulate the existence, in the time of the end brought about by the advent of the nuclear age, of two distinct and irreconcilable sides, the culprits and the victims. It is not suicide we are dealing with, but the murder of one part of the species by another part of the same species.[12] At the same time, nuclear technology being what it is, annihilation would eventually extend to all humans indistinctly, so that, according to him, "fission" would dialectically pass over into "fusion": "the effect of nuclear war will no longer bear any trace of duality, as the enemies will constitute a one and only vanquished humankind" (Ibid.: 79). Thus, as in Chakrabarty, it seems that there will only be *one* humankind when there is *none* – when the last human being has vanished from the face of the Earth.[13]

In the context of climate catastrophe that defines the Anthropocene, the line separating victims and culprits is, as we have seen, historically clear from a collective or societal point of view, but much harder to trace from the point of view of individual action. This is because, today, many of us (us humans, and the non-humans we have enslaved or colonized) are victims and culprits "all at once," in each action we engage in, at the push of every button, with every portion of food or animal feed we swallow – even if it is as obvious as it is essential that we do not confuse McDonald's itself with the teenager conditioned into consuming junk food, or Monsanto with the small farmer obliged to spray his genetically modified corn with glyphosate, let alone the pharmaceutical industry with the cattle force-fed with antibiotics and hormones.[14] Even if, as with the nuclear apocalypse, all of us at any rate will, some sooner, some later, become victims of the crossing of "planetary boundaries," this does not prevent us from identifying the opposing camps, as Latour points out now and Anders (2007: 33) himself suggested: "The time of the end in which we live (...) contains two kinds of men: culprits and victims. We should take this duality into account: the name of our work is 'combat'."[15]

Anders defends what he calls "prophylactic apocalypticism." In a similar line of reasoning to that of his friend Hans Jonas' (1985: 26–7) "heuristics of fear," he explains:

> If we distinguish ourselves from classic Judeo-Christian apocalyptics, it is not only because we fear the end (which they, in turn, hoped for), but above all because our apocalyptic passion has no other goal than to prevent the apocalypse. *We are apocalyptic only so we can be wrong.* (Anders 2007: 29–30; our emphasis)

In that sense, the prophecy of "the end of the world" must be performatively announced so that it will *not* come true – which suggests, we should note in passing, a wholly different way of interpreting Chakrabarty's idea of "negative universal history."[16] *It is our duty to be pessimistic*, that is Anders' fundamental message, at once anticipating Clive Hamilton's (2010) argument about the present environmental crisis and contradicting the stance taken by Latour in a recent interview ("it is my duty to be optimistic"; Latour 2013c).[17] The author of *Le temps de la fin*, in short, calls for a veritable *political* combat, a "war" in the sense that Latour will borrow from Carl Schmitt, a "toxic" author who was Anders' ideological antipode: war as strictly immanent conflict, where there is no possible intervention from an external arbiter or superior authority, in which it is necessary to confront the enemy in a scenario where the physical annihilation ("existential negation") of the other is a real possibility. We have seen that, for Chakrabarty, the two actors conjured by the Anthropocene are the human species and the Earth, but, even though humans have become a natural force on a geological scale, and the "Earth System" has taken on the unpredictable behavior that we attribute to beasts (the climate beast...), the conflict appears to have a clear arbiter, which is Science: climatology, geophysics, natural history. If we wish to survive the Anthropocene, Chakrabarty seems to say, it is to this transcendent instance that we have to pay heed and obedience. In Anders' nuclear apocalypse, on the contrary, if we can say that there will be no instance exterior to the interested parties, it is because *all* are either *on the side of* the murderers or *on the side of the* victims, but also because, at the same time, *all will ultimately be victims*, including the world in which the conflict will unfold. As in Lars von Trier's *Melancholia*, there will be no voiceover left to narrate the end of history. The absence of a transcendent entity that could save us from the apocalypse – benevolent Martians worried about the evolution of the Cold War, for instance – is dwarfed by the absence of a world after total nuclear conflagration. The end of atomic war would be the absolute end of the world and the absolute end of humankind.

Anders thus spoke of a combat at "the time of the end" in order to push back "the end of times" – a political combat for peace, so as to prevent a war which, paradoxically (and here is another parallel with the Anthropocene), *had already begun*, having come into existence since the construction of the first atomic bomb became a concrete possibility – and which, we should remember, has for the same reason still not ended. Bruno Latour (2013a), in turn, while also speaking of a war that has already started, stresses that this war must be "officially" declared before peace talks can begin, not only in order to avoid the "end of the world" through the generalization of ecocide that follows the expansion of the modernization front, but also to create or *institute* a world, a "common world" to be more precise, a *modus vivendi* among the inhabitants of a planet heretofore placed under the sign of Gaia, a "divine character" (*theoteros*) very dissimilar to Nature or Divinity in the modern period. A character that above all has no *interest* in acting as external arbiter in the conflict between the two peoples, the two opposing *demoi* engaged in a struggle to the death around the *nomos* (order, distribution, appropriation) of the Earth.[18]

For some time now, Latour has been collecting evidence of the objective historical crumbling of the distinction that founds modernity: that between nature and politics. More recently, he has indicated planetary environmental collapse as at once the most real result and the most eloquent proof of the unreality of that distinction – which creates a situation that we could describe as the multiple organ failure of the cosmopolitical government (*nomos*) of the Moderns. In his 2013 Gifford Lectures, the relation between the two poles of "humankind" (*anthropos* as *demos*) and "world" ("Nature" as *theos*, but also the world as ordered/appropriated by modernity) is subjected to a detailed analysis. Crucially, they are reconstructed in terms that seek above all to highlight the fractured, divided, untotalizable, polemical, contingent – in a word: political – character of *both* actants, and the resulting impossibility of dividing them *as such* into two homogeneous opposing camps. The two mythical characters of our text merge here into a single-sided figure: humankind is not on the other side of Being; it is not the world's reverse or negative, just as the world is not the "context" (the "environment") of a Subject that counter-defines it as Object. It is not this duality that counts; nor is this the negativity that imposes itself.

However, it is exactly for that reason that it is necessary to recognize that we are at war. If the falling apart of the modern "Constitution" was already visible to the naked eye, as is attested by the proposal of an ontological reform of modernity long developed by Latour and finally presented in his *An Inquiry into Modes of Existence* (2013d), the climate crisis – a subtle but insistent undercurrent running across that book, brought to the fore in its closing pages – has given this war a character of urgency, placing us before the imperative of practically determining who are these "all," against whom exactly the war is being waged, and which side "we" are on. The path to a desired future universal peace can only be walked, as Latour sees it, if we start by a multiple and combined refusal of the present cosmopolitical assemblage (*demos-theos-nomos*) instituted by the Moderns. Refusal, then, of the precocious cosmopolitical unification of the multiverse (that is, a refusal of the unification of the "world," this multinatural space of coexistence for planes of immanence traced by the numberless collectives that traverse and animate it); refusal of the separation of and precedence of fact over value, given over constructed, natural over artificial, nature over culture; refusal of the power of police ascribed to Science as the sole authorized intermediary of first Nature; refusal of the only "true" fetishism, to wit, the self-referentiality of the Economy as the science of second Nature, with its pretension to measuring values that are in fact established by the measuring activity itself. Refusal, finally, of the idea of *anthropos* as a prematurely unified entity, a figure that eclipses the contradictory and heterogeneous plurality of conditions and interests of the collectives that are faced with Gaia's daunting theophany in the name, once again, of a Nature – "human nature," this strange amalgam of the first and second Natures contrasted in *An Inquiry into Modes of Existence*.

So we can follow the "political theology" argument developed by Latour in the Gifford Lectures, which are a postface of sorts to *An Inquiry*, we should begin by taking up once more the "world" pole of our mythical macro-scheme. The author entreats us to witness an ongoing historical transition (and to fight for its completion) between two images of the world: the modern Earth of Galilean science, a heavenly body among others that wanders across an isotropic and infinite universe in conformity to the eternal laws of mathematics; and Lovelock's and Margulis's Gaia, an exceptional local region in the universe, a cosmical accident created by life's geomorphic agency, whose physico-chemical contribution to the constitution of a far-from-equilibrium system was and is determinant for the continuation of life itself. The macrophysical agency of humans on which Chakrabarty rightly insists is, therefore, only one example, though an admittedly disastrous one for humans and other living beings in the present geological epoch, of this ontological inseparability of ground and form, of "the living" and its "environment." What Isabelle Stengers (2015) has aptly named "intrusion of Gaia" marks a decisive event in this *hapax* that is Lovelock's Gaia, the advent of a *novel* historical situation in which it has become definitively impossible to live without taking into account the *meaning* of this inseparability.

Gaia-Earth thus detaches itself from Heavenly Body-Earth, the sublunary becomes once more distinct from the superlunary, and the idea of "world" recovers a radically closed sense, which is also to say that it becomes immanent: terrestrial, local, proximate, secular, non-unified. The expression "this sublunary realm of ours" (or "sublunar oikos of Gaia") is recurrent throughout the Gifford Lectures, always appearing in contexts in which the author differentiates between the situation of universal legality (*quid juris?*) of Nature, such as asserted by relativity or quantum mechanics[19] – a legality that Latour does not refuse as such, but only as a mystical emanation of a disembodied model of Science as supreme arbiter, mystical oracle supposedly come to dethrone the old Deities – and the situation of empirical entanglement that we could name, for once without pejorative connotations, *Terran exceptionalism.*[20] It is here that we can see the full political significance of the choice presented by Paul Ennis (2013) between the cosmocentrism of speculative realists, "deterritorializers" who are firmly reterritorialized in Big Science (the physico-mathematical knowledge and techno-economic dispositif of access to what is farthest from us), and the geocentrism of "continental philosophy," represented in Latour's case by a passion for "small sciences" (Terran sciences in the double sense of being *close to home* – proximate knowledges concerning the soil, the climate, ecology, the city – and of being *secular*, that is, engaging nature as an internal, multiple, animate, the perpetually *in fieri* correlate of the concrete activity of scientists). Implications that Isabelle Stengers (2013b) has perhaps managed to make explicit even more radically than Latour with her notion of "slow science." For the *only* thing we need to accelerate, in light of the "coming barbarism," is precisely the process of slowing down the sciences and the civilization that instrumentalizes them (Stengers 2013b, 2015).

Even though it is essentially animate – as in a fairy tale, where each object can cut itself off from the background in order to become an actor in the proscenium – Latour's Gaia is not a *super*-animate entity, a mysterious all-powerful Eminence, a super-organism endowed with a puzzling type of intentionality that would be akin to the balanced resultant of all the forces acting in its bosom, which would suppose an Engineer or Governor that would just distribute the roles and functions of previously existing "parts," coordinating them through feedback loops.[21] In Latour's reinterpretation (or scientific portrait, we could say with a Deleuzian wink) of Lovelock, Gaia is a gigantic discordant harmony, mutable and contingent, "a mess" (2013a: 68) of multiple intentionalities distributed among all agents. Each organism manipulates its environment "to render its own survival slightly less improbable" (Ibid.: 67). That dissolves the opposition between inside and outside, organism and environment, since the environment of each organism, and therefore of all organisms, are all other organisms (the environment as a society of societies, as in the Amerindian world?); their entangled intentionalities constitute overlapping "waves of action" (as in Tarde's monads?) in perpetual cycles of ebb and flow, expansion and contraction. If Gaia is also a *living* and *plural* world, as in the Edenic image of the wilderness, it is not a *harmonious* or *balanced* one, let alone dependent for its existence on the exclusion of humankind, as if the latter were an extraterrestrial invader come to spoil a pastoral idyll. The Edenic world is a world without history (the latter only beginning, precisely, with the Fall), whereas Gaia is first and foremost made of history, it is *history materialized*, a contingent and tumultuous sequence of events rather than the unfolding of a "superlunary" causality following timeless laws. In Latour's conception, thus, it is not so much the case that human history comes to an unexpected fusion with geohistory; rather, it is Gaia-Earth that becomes historicized, narrativized as human history[22] – with which it shares, and this caveat is essential, the absence of any intervention from whatever kind of Providence.

What we still need to work out is who is the *demos* of Gaia, the people that this entity gathers and convokes, and who their enemy is. As stated above, we must begin by rejecting any sole candidate to the (in)dignity of being the Anthropocene's eponymous. The Wilsonian notion of species is dismissed less on the grounds of its phenomenological eva-nescence, as in Chakrabarty, than because it is a tributary of modernity's apolitical, ahistorical conception of Nature, as well as of Science's absolute power of arbitrage. But neither are the revolutionary masses of the classical left, that other recurring incarnation of the modern universal, up to the task; if the latter-day priests of the philosophy of praxis are to be believed, their liberation continues to depend on a general-ization and intensification of the modernization front, on the practical (environmental destruction) as well as theoretical (the cult of Nature and Reason) levels. What the Anthro-pocene pre-empts is precisely the notion of an *anthropos*, a universal subject (species, *but also* class or multitude) capable of acting as a single *people*. The properly *ethnopolitical* situ-ation of "human" as intensive and extensive multiplicity of *peoples* must be acknowledged as being directly implicated in the Anthropocene crisis. If there is no positive human interest, it is because there is a diversity of political alignments among the various world peoples or "cultures" with several other non-human actants and peoples (constituting what Latour calls "collectives") *against* the self-appointed spokespeople of universal Human. The multiverse, the ante-nomic or pre-cosmic background state, remains non-unified, on the human as well as on the world side. All unification lies in the future, under what we could call a multiple hypothetical mode, and will depend on negotiating capacities once the "war of the worlds," as Latour has called it elsewhere, has been declared.

§ In this older text by Latour (2002), "war of the worlds" made reference above all to the relations between the Moderns and other peoples along the so-called "modernization front." Assured of their privileged access to Nature, Moderns saw themselves as a civilizing force come to convince recalcitrant peoples to rally to the flag of a common world (a single ontological and cosmo-political regime) that was also, not by coincidence, the world of the Moderns. In the face of the increasingly apparent signs of the collapse of the "Constitution" (the cosmopolitics) that had guided them for over 300 years, Latour presented himself then as a diplomat representing the Moderns, which would help them to compose a true peace and a true unity to come, on the condition that they acknowledged the existence of a veritable war there where they could only see a matter of policing and "resocializing" ontological delinquents (namely, non-Moderns). Thirteen years later, in the closing pages of *An Inquiry into Modes of Existence*, the author discusses the emergence of two new, unexpected fronts that could maybe convince Moderns of the need to negotiate peace: the first was the evidence that, in the East and in the South, other peoples had learned their lesson too well, taking upon themselves the will and the responsibility for modernization, but in their own, frightful terms; the second was the "irruption of Gaia," the hypersensible nature of the Anthropocene, a strange enemy whose existence we need to acknowledge if we are to have any possibility of surviving as a civilization. In the Gifford Lectures, finally, Latour redefines the two opposing camps as "Humans" (the Moderns who believe it will be possible to go on living in the unified, indifferent Nature of the Holocene) and "Terrans" (the people of Gaia), even though he also sometimes refers to a war between Humans and Gaia, which therefore appears the enemy of Humans proper (Latour 2013a: 121–2).

The Gaia War is a war of the worlds, and not a conflict about the present and future state of the planetary body called Earth, because we are not discussing if there are such things as global warming and an ongoing environmental collapse; these are among the best-documented – "referenced" in Latour's (2013d) sense – phenomena in the history of sciences. We are not dealing with a *matter of fact*, since there is hardly any significant controversy among scientists concerning the anthropic origin of climate catastrophe. Certainly, that does not stop segments of public opinion, academia included – not to mention governments, big corporations, and their "mer-chants of doubt" (Oreskes and Conway 2010) – from questioning that consensus and insisting on business as usual, nor does it dampen green capitalist optimism about "crisis as opportunity."[23] That this is so is because the rationalist theory of action (from establishing facts to discussing the measures to be taken and finally to taking action) does not function in such cases where matters of fact and matters of concern prove themselves to be indissolubly entangled, as the Cold War's nuclear crisis made perfectly obvious. What is at stake in environmental controversy are positions in which actors are *politically* implicated, where some have everything to lose while others have a lot to gain, which entails that the distinction between "fact" and "value" has, precisely, no value whatsoever.[24] It is a *civil war* situation, and not a police operation exercised from a point of legitimate authority, in order to bring delinquents "back to reason" through application of the Law. It is, in short, a matter of deciding *what world we want to live in*:

> [A]re the statements about ecological conflicts more like "the boiling point of water" or more like "the Cold War threat"? In other words, are we dealing with a world made of distant matters of fact or a world composed of highly reactive matters of concern? This too divides sharply since those on both sides of the border, literally, do not inhabit the same world. To put it too starkly: some are readying themselves to live as Earthbound in the Anthropocene; other decided to remain as Humans in the Holocene. (Latour 2013a: 11)

That does not mean, we suppose, that being correctly informed of the knowledge that the pertinent sciences have been producing about global warming cannot be an important factor in bringing "Humans" over to the Terran side – as has in fact increasingly been the case.

Yet if the Terrans of the Anthropocene cannot be confused with the human species as a whole, would that entail that the People of Gaia form a part of that species, and that species alone? Terrans are the party toward which Latour seems inclined, the one he seeks to evoke and convoke in his lectures in political theology.[25] Ontologically and politically tied to the Earth's cause, Terrans are today up in arms, although Latour (2013a: 118ff) hopes, in a strange repetition of Carl Schmitt, that they "might be the 'artisans of peace'" against the ambiguous and treacherous Humans. These are,

it is well understood, none other than the *Moderns*, that race
– originally North-Western, but increasingly less European
and more Chinese, Indian, Brazilian – which twice denied the
Earth: first by defining itself as technologically exempt from
nature's trials, then by defining itself as the only civilization
to have escaped the closed (but dangerous and unpredictable)
world of archaic animisms, the only one that opened itself
up to the infinite (but saturated with imperturbable necessity)
universe of inanimate matter.

But the author of *We Have Never Been Modern* does not
seem too sure what to think about his Terrans. At times
they are conceived as an emerging network of independent
Latourian scientists (as opposed to modernist scientists and
their corporate backers), practicing a "fully incarnated"
(Latour 2013a: 120), dynamic, politicized science that is ori-
ented toward our sublunary realm; they represent "the small,
the tiny source of hope" (Ibid.: 121) that the author is not
entirely convinced we should still hold on to ("it is my *duty*
to be optimistic"...). At other times, Terrans appear as the
name of a *common cause*, which concerns all of the planet's
collectives, but which can only properly come together if
future ex-Moderns make their anxiously anticipated vow of
humility and open up a space for cosmopolitical dialogue:

> If the multiverse is reintroduced and if the natural sciences
> are relocated inside it, is it possible to let the other collectives
> stop being "cultures" and give them full access to reality by
> letting them compose their cosmos, but by using other keys,
> other modes of extension than the one allowed by knowledge
> production?[26] Such a reinterpretation is especially relevant
> today because, if nature is not universal, climates have always
> been important to all people. The reintroduction of climates
> and atmospheres as the new common cosmopolitical concern
> gives a new urgency to this communality between collectives.
> (Latour 2013a: 50).

A throw of the dice of the "common world" will therefore
never abolish the multiverse. It is less a matter of theoretical
universality than of practical interest, a question of *subsistence*. The climate, that variable and fluctuating thing par
excellence, becomes the element of historico-political syn-
chronization of the interest of all the world's peoples. What

the weather is like becomes *what counts* (in) the flow of time.[27] In that respect, Latour's "common world" is the opposite of a "world without us" in the sense of a universe without anyone, a cosmos unified by the absence of experience, by the unreality of everything that is not figure and movement.

However, as we have pointed out, our author hesitates when it comes to identifying his Terrans.[28] In the fifth conference, he identifies these "people bound to the Earth" with the two human characters in Béla Tarr's *The Turin Horse*, perpetually condemned to survive – one should really say *sub*vive – on an Earth that progressively loses its worldly condition.[29] We must confess that this move strikes us as a terribly enigmatic one. It would no doubt be reasonable to take the deadly monotony that crushes the film's protagonists as an eloquent metaphor of the condition of so many indigenous peoples around the world after the modernization front crossed their lives.[30] (Or maybe, as some have argued, as an allegory of the shameful debacle of socialism.) In that case, however, we should not forget to note the fleeting flash of a solitary and incongruous ray of joy in the film, brought and carried away by the gipsy cart that noisily turns up at the farm to ask for water and then travels on, presenting the female protagonist (who, invited to come with them, declines) with a mysterious book that talks about the closing and demolition of churches.[31] Maybe those gypsies (one should pause to think what it means to be a gypsy in Hungary these days...) are the true anticipatory image of the Terran vanguard, capable of leading the war against Humans all the way to its decisive moments. For it is difficult to conceive the People of Gaia as a Majority, as the universalization of European good conscience; Terrans cannot but be an "irremediably minor" people, however numerous they may come to be, a people that would never mistake the territory for the Earth.[32] In that regard, they probably resemble less the "phantom public" of Western democracies (Latour 2008) than the *people that is missing* which Deleuze and Guattari speak of: Kafka and Melville's minor people, Rimbaud's inferior race, the Indian that the philosopher becomes ("perhaps 'so that' the Indian who is himself Indian becomes something else and tears himself away from his own agony") – the people, that is, to come; capable of launching a "resistance to the present" and thus of creating "a new earth," the world to come (Deleuze and Guattari 1994: 108–9).[33]

The end of the world as a fractal event

I do not want to die again
Davi Kopenawa

Further into his account, Latour (2013a: 126) wonders whether it would not be possible to "accept the candidacy of those people who claim to be assembled, for instance, by Pachamama, the Earth goddess." He is obviously referring to Amerindian peoples and their fellow non-Moderns, who have increasingly adapted Western environmental rhetoric to their cosmologies, conceptual vocabularies, and existential projects, and re-translated the latter into a modernized language whose political intent is unequivocal and has started to make itself heard by the citizens of privileged societies in the "global North" – at least by those who have realized that, this time, things will turn out bad for everyone, everywhere. Latour, however, does not think that these "people of Pachamama" are really up to the task:

> Maybe, if only we could be sure that what passes for a respect for the Earth is not due to their small numbers and to the relative weakness of their technology. None of those so called "traditional" people, the wisdom of which we often admire, is prepared to scale up their ways of life to the size of the giant technical metropolises in which are now corralled more than half of the human race. (Latour 2013a: 128)

It seems to us that Latour fails to consider the possibility that the generally small populations and "relatively weak" technologies of indigenous peoples and so many other sociopolitical minorities of the Earth could become a crucial advantage and resource in a post-catastrophic time, or, if one wishes, in a *permanently* diminished human world. Our author does not seem prepared, himself, to accept the highly likely possibility that *we* – the people of the (capitalist) Core, the overweight, mediatically controlled, psychopharmacologically stabilized automata of technologically "advanced" societies that are highly dependent on a monumental con-sumption (or rather, waste) of energy – that we, when the chips are down, might be the ones who will have to *scale down* our precious ways of living.[34] As a matter of fact, if someone needs "to be prepared" for something, that someone is us, the ones who are crowded together in "giant technical metropolises."

The opposition between Moderns and non-Moderns, developed in Latour's seminal *We Have Never Been Modern*, largely depended on the idea of a "difference of scale," that is, the difference in length of sociotechnical networks in these two regimes of collectives. In his proposal for a new Con-stitution, Latour's concern was precisely with how to retain the "long networks" of modern collectives, considered as an undeniable historical step forward. But given that the Anthro-pocene consists in the collapse of scalar magnitudes, when the species as biological agent becomes species as geophysi-cal force (through the historical mediation of the "species" as thaumaturgical engineer), when political economy meets cosmic entropy, it is the very idea of scale and dimension that seems out of scale. After all, is it not Latour himself who observes, in the same conferences, that "[n]othing [is] at the right scale"? What do we know about the expansion and reduction of scales we will have to undergo in the course of this century? Not much. The future is ever less certain, better (or worse) still, what can be known about it is only that, as the song goes, "nothing will be like before."[35]

As for the small population of "so-called traditional" peoples, there are in fact around 370 million indigenous people – members of collectives that are not recognized, nor do they recognize themselves, as standard citizens of the nation-states that encompass and often divide them – spread over 70 countries in the world, according to a recent United Nations Permanent Forum on Indigenous Issues (2009) esti-mate. This is certainly nowhere near the roughly 3.5 billion people (read half the human species) crowding our "technical metropolises," around a billion of which, it should be noted, live in not particularly "technical" slums (Davis 2006).[36] Still, it is more than the population of the United States (314 million) and Canada (35 million) put together, which surely must be worth something. Above all, however, who knows what demographic transitions await humankind before the end of this century, or even earlier, if we consider that we could arrive at a 4°C increase in temperature already by 2060 or 2070 (Betts et al. 2011)? Not to mention the well-known argument according to which five Earths would be required if all the 7 billion human inhabitants of the planet adopted that bizarre Modern version of *vivir bien*[37] that is the American way of life. That means that the country to the north of Mexico owes the rest of the world at least four worlds, in an unexpected transformation of the mythical "humans without world" theme. Apart from there being too many people in the world (unfortunately, no amount of rationalization can unmake that evidence), the problem above all is that there are too few people with too much world, and too many people with way too little.

Plus intra is Latour's plea (2013a: 129–30) against this danger, a correction to and necessary update of the *plus ultra* that was the motto from the Age of Discoveries – which, let us not forget, *instituted* the modern "*nomos* of the Earth" which required the American genocide and, more generally, the extermination of several millions of human beings that lay outside the *jus gentium* of Europe, and thus in the legitimately appropriable, up-for-grabs "free zones" of the globe.[38] According to Latour, it is now imperative that we recognize the existence of limits ("Terrans must explore the question of their limits…"[39]); that we let the idea sink that every action in this sublunary realm of ours has a cost, that is, consequences that inevitably act back on the agent. [40] Latour's motto evidently strikes us as most sensible. (Tarde, as we have seen, had already advanced in his *Fragment* a really radical version of it…) We interpret it nonetheless as a plea for us to prepare for a *non-material intensification*[41] of our "way of life," which is to say, a total transformation thereof, in a process that should definitely steer clear of any fantasy of "Promethean mastery" or managerial control over the world understood as humankind's Other. The time has come to transform *enkrateia*, the mastery of oneself, into a *collective* project of re-civilization – "civilizing modern practices," writes Stengers (2013b: 113) – or maybe a more "molecular," less titanic project, of *uncivilization*.[42] *Plus intra* must mean, in that sense, a *technology of slowing down*, a *diseconomy* no longer mesmerized by the hallucination of continuous growth, a *cultural insurrection* (if the expression may be pardoned) against the zombiefication of the citizen-consumer.

One word on technology. We believe it is necessary to do the same in relation to Technology and technologies that Latour has done in relation to the fateful amalgam of Science and sciences: rejecting the unidirectional, modernist understanding of Technology that regards it as an onto-anthropological essence whose triumphant deployment blossoms across history. (Breakthrough Institute-style technophiles are as essentialist as their retro-Heideggerean enemies.) For there are Human and Terran technologies, a difference that we do not think is reducible to the mere issue of network length. The war between Humans and Terrans will essentially take place at this level, especially when we bring under an enlarged and pluralized category of technology, a whole series of recent sociotechnical detours and institutional inventions, some very ancient, others quite recent, from the kinship systems and totemic maps of Australian aboriginals to the horizontal organization and the defensive Black Bloc tactics of alterglobalist movements, from the forms of production, circulation, mobilization, and communication created by the internet (Wark 2004) to the organizations who protect and exchange traditional seeds and plants in zones of peasant resistance all over the world, from efficient extra-banking financial transfer systems like *hawala* to the differential arboriculture of the Amazonian indigenous and to Polynesian stellar navigation, from the "experimental agriculturalists" of the Brazilian semi-arid (see ASPTA 2013) to hypercontemporaneous innovations such as ecovillages, from the psychopolitics of technoshamanism to the decentralized economies of social currencies, bitcoin, and crowdsourcing.[43] Not every technical innovation key to the resilience of the species needs to go through the corporate channels of Big Science or the very long human and non-human networks mobilized by "cutting-edge" technologies. That is, as a matter of fact, something that Latour himself does not fail to recognize in *An Inquiry into Modes of Existence*:

> If the verb "ecologize" is to become an alternative to "modernize," we shall need to establish quite different transactions

with technological beings. (…) The Australian aborigines whose toolbox contained only a few poor artifacts – made of stone, horn, or skin – nevertheless knew how to establish with technological beings relations of a complexity that continues to stun archaeologists: *the differentials of resistance that they arranged were located rather in the tissue of myths and the subtle texture of kinship bonds and landscapes.* The fact that their materiality was slight in the colonizers' eyes tells us nothing about the inventiveness, the resistance, and the durability of these arrangements. *To keep open opportunities for negotiation over the successors of the contemporary production arrangements, it is crucial to restore to the beings of technology a capacity for combination that liberates them entirely from the heavy weight of instrumentality. Freedom of maneuver that is indispensable in order to invent the arrangements to be set up when we have to dismantle the impossible modernization front.* (2013d: 231; our italics)

In *An Inquiry*'s online version, the author adds a note on this unexpected relationship between the aboriginals' "Neolithic" technology and the future unmaking of the modernization front, or what we call the non-material intensification of our way of life. He makes it clear that his *"Plus intra"* is meant as a non-accelerationist, non-techno-triumphalist position regarding the new *nomos* of the Earth:

> The anthropology of techniques, ethnotechnology and ethnoarchaeology have, each in their own way, multiplied alternative descriptions allowing us to separate technology from the narrow ethnocentric repertoire of production, labor, "material base," without losing any of the very particular objectivity involved in the encounter with TEC beings.[44]

Not to mention the interesting possibility, for now as fictional as the Singularitarians' dreams, that the meta-universal machines of the future themselves, the improved avatars in which we will (re)incarnate in the techno-mystical fusion that will create Cosmic Man, will be endowed with artificial intelligence that is sufficiently astute to resist the natural stupidity of humans, opting for a mechanopolitics of intensive sufficiency:

> It's called the Mauldin Test. One sign of whether an artificial entity is truly intelligent may be when it decides, abruptly, to

stop cooperating with AI acceleration. *Not* to design its successor. To slow things down. Enough to live. Just live. (David
Brin 2012: 448)

As if machines had finally became capable of resynthesiz-
ing, *motu proprio*, Caetano Veloso's prophetic vision of the
figure to come of the Terran, namely, the Indian: the one
who is – because he was, because he always will have been –
"more advanced than the most advanced of most advanced
technologies."[45]

To Terran technologies we should add, finally, the vast
repertoire of technical detours mobilized by Darwinian evolution in organisms. *Pace* Latour (2013d: ch. 8), we think
technologies do not historically and ontologically precede
humans *only* because they have made them, and made them
as *Homo faber*. Bricolage, tinkering, the hack, the crack, the
exploit – all of these are anthropogenetic to the extent that
they are *inherent to the living*. To borrow the language of *An
Inquiry into Modes of Existence*, the REP.TEC crossing has
been practiced by living beings for millions of years; it might
even be what allows us to differentiate, within the universal
mode REP, the trajectory of so-called "animate" and "inanimate" existents. Reciprocally, we know that several "technical choices" made by humans have caused or may cause the
species' REP extinction without any possibility of "starting
over several times" (that possibility being what defines TEC,
according to Latour). Nuclear war technology is the most
obvious example, though by far not the only one. What are
the present environmental crisis and the threat that it repre-
sents to all humans, if not the consequences of numberless
"technical choices"? And how many of them will allow for
a "starting over," a second "chance"?[46]

Once we accept this enlarged definition of "technique" or
"technology," it is possible to see with greater clarity that the
division between Humans and Terrans is not only internal to
our species. (That, we suppose, is something Latour would
easily agree with.) The Gaia War opposes two camps or sides
populated by humans and non-humans – micro-organisms,
animals, plants, machines, rivers, glaciers, oceans, chemical elements, and compounds. In short, the whole range of
existents that find themselves implicated in the advent of

the Anthropocene, and whose persistence (with their specific "trajectories," "hiatuses," "passes," and "felicity conditions"; see Latour 2013d) is virtually or actually posed as the "negation" of the opposing camp, or is "negated" by it – in short, in the Schmittian position of the *political enemy*.[47] The lethal viruses propagated by equally damaging intercontinental tourism; the vast symbiotic fauna of bacteria that have coevolved with humans; the lethal bacteria that have become definitively resistant to antibiotics;[48] the atomic weapons silently awaiting their hour in underground silos and perpetually mobile submarines; the uncountable legion of confined and mistreated animals in extermination camps for the extraction of protein (Foer 2010); the powerful methane factories located in the stomachs of billions of human-raised ruminants in industrial farms; the floods and devastating droughts caused by global warming; the Aral Sea that is no more; the tens of thousands of species becoming extinct every year (at a rate perhaps 1,000 times higher than the average rate of extinction on the evolutionary scale; see Kolbert 2014); the accelerated deforestation of the Amazon and of Indonesia; the damming of the Amazonian Basin to produce hydroelectric energy, with very likely nefarious, if not catastrophic, effects for the macro-region; the saturation of arable soils by pesticides produced by Bayer and BASF, two of the honorable successors of IG Farben, whose history hardly needs recounting; the brave *Amaranthus palmeri*, the "Inca amaranth" that resists Monsanto's RoundUp herbicide and spreads into transgenic soya plantations; the Terminator seeds produced by that same detestable corporation, which invades traditional corn, manioc, rice, or millet plantations carefully preserved by peasants in zones that resist the encroachment of agribusiness; the many mysterious chemical additives in our food; pets and police dogs; the grizzlies that lose their patience with humans who cannot respect the difference between species; the irreplaceable bee people at risk of disappearing by virtue of a synergy of anthropic factors; killer drones, the melting permafrost, the internet, GPS satellites, the paraphernalia of scientific instruments, models, and experiments that allow us to evaluate the progress of planetary boundaries – in short, all these countless agents, agencies, actants, actors, acts, phenomena, or however else one may wish to call them are automatically enlisted in the Gaia War, some or maybe many of which may change camps (function, effects) in the most unexpected ways, and which enter into articulations with different peoples, collectives, and organizations of individuals of the *Homo sapiens* species, which oppose each other precisely by dint of the alliances that they establish and maintain with this non-human multitude, that is, of the vital interests that connect them to their "others."

While it is not too difficult to list the non-humans that are involved in this war, we have seen that it is not as easy to identify *within* the human species who the Terrans are and who are their "Human" enemies. We have seen that the latter are rather generically associated by Latour with the "Moderns," that is, all those agents, from corporations to countries and individuals, which are implicated in some way or another (and the difference among modes of implication is, it bears repeating, essential) in the implacable advance of the modernization front. Yet it is neither impossible nor useless to name at least some of those on the frontlines of the "Human" army, those who are most immediately responsible for the accelerating worsening of anthropocenic catastrophe and more directly interested (or uninterested?) in the defeat of the Terrans. After all, just for starters, only 90 big companies are responsible for *two thirds* of greenhouse gas emissions into the Earth's atmosphere: Chevron, Exxon, BP, Shell, Saudi Aramco, Russian Gazprom, Norway's Statoil, Brazil's Petrobrás, the coal and mining state companies of countries such as China, Russia, Poland....[49] Right after those, names like Monsanto, Dupont, Syngenta, Bayer, Cargill, Bunge, Dow, Rio Tinto, Nestlé, "our very own" Brazilian Vale, the companies belonging to the sinister Koch brothers, and several others also deserve a mention for their various contributions to the conversion of the Moderns' cosmological "mononaturalism" into a large-scale agricultural economy of monocultures, to the lasting perturbation of the geochemical cycles of soil and water, to massive environmental pollution, to the dissemination of food that is harmful to human health...[50] We should not forget the 147 banks and other corporations, the tentacles of whose super-network involves the planet in a deadly embrace (see Coghlan and MacKenzie 2011)...Nor the governments of countries like Canada, Australia, the United States, Brazil, and several others that have stimulated deforestation and the extraction of fuels and minerals with high contaminating potentials, as well as created obstacles for negotiations around the climate catastrophe...It is a long list, to be sure, but certainly not an infinite one. It is not against "civilization," "progress," "history," "destiny," or "human-kind" that Terrans are fighting, but against these entities acting *on behalf* of Humans.

Yet let us go back to our elusive Terrans, considering again for an instant the Amerindian cosmogonies and eschatologies evoked earlier on, when we spoke of their aesthetic anthropomorphism and metaphysical panpsychism. In a world where "everything is alive," it is necessary to account for death. Indigenous myths see the origin of culture and society as being intrinsically bound with the origin of humans' short lifespan, that is, of their mortality as existential condition. The latter is commonly imagined as the result, not of a crime or a sin against divinity, but of a blunder, a mistake, some careless act of unexplainable stupidity on the part of our ancestors. Archaic humans made the wrong choice when confronted with certain alternatives offered by the demiurge, the consequence of which is aging and dying quickly, as opposed to living forever like other beings (rocks, hardwood trees) or remaining forever young through periodic changes of skin, like reptiles and various invertebrates. On top of that, post-mythical speciation being derived from an originary intensive continuum of "human" consistency, inter- and intra-cultural distinctions among presently existing humans are usually explained as resulting from demographic impoverishment – in other words, from the high death rate inflicted on an excessively large and homogeneous population (extinction by catastrophe, extermination by a divinity) (Lévi-Strauss 1975), which produced "holes" and distances that allowed for the diversification of humankind into categorially discrete peoples, tribes, and clans.

Yet none of this is seen as entirely negative, even if we might lament our ancestors' foolishness. After all, if people did not die, there would not be enough space in which to raise and feed future generations. "How could we have children, if we lived forever and the world were saturated with

people? Where would they live, what would they eat?," These
are the kinds of comments that the narrators of these myths
normally make. Now, if Amerindians, like so many other
non-Modern peoples, share some sort of fundamental cultural goal, it is that of *having children*, constituting groups
of relatives, allying themselves through marriage to other
groups of relatives, distributing and disseminating themselves
through their descendants, for people live *in* other people,
with other people, *for* other people (Sahlins 2013). Ultimately, Indians prefer to maintain a relatively stable population instead of increasing "productivity" and "improving"
technology in order to create conditions ("surplus") so that
there can always be more people, more needs, more concerns.
The ethnographic present of slow societies contains an image
of their future. Indians are Malthusians in their own way.

It is not possible to know for sure whether these myths
precede the Conquest, but that is in all likelihood the case.
Indigenous imagination had already started to think the
reduction or slowing down of their Anthropocene, except
they placed the process at the origin rather than the end
of the world. Little could they imagine then, perhaps, that
their world would soon be taken away from them by those
world-forming, world-destroying aliens, the Europeans. Be as
it may, what we hinted above, that indigenous people have
something to teach us when it comes to apocalypses, losses
of world, demographic catastrophes, and ends of History,
means simply this: for the native people of the Americas, *the
end of the world already happened* – five centuries ago. To
be exact, it began on October 12, 1492. (As someone once
said on Twitter, "the first Indian to find Columbus made a
horrible discovery"...) The indigenous population of the
continent, larger than that of Europe at the time, may have
lost – by means of the combined action of viruses (smallpox
in particular being spectacularly lethal), iron, gunpowder,
and paper (treaties, papal bulls, royal *encomienda* conces-
sions, and of course the Bible) – something of the order of
95 percent of its bulk throughout the first one and a half
centuries of the Conquest. That would correspond, according to some demographers, to a fifth of the planet's population.[51] We could therefore call this American event the First
Great Modern Extinction, when the New World was hit by

the Old one as if by a giant celestial body that we could call, by analogy with Lars von Trier's Melancholia, planet Commodity.[52] If it comes to comparing apocalypses, we can safely say that the American genocide of the sixteenth and seventeenth centuries – the biggest demographic catastrophe in History until now, with the possible exception of the Black Death – will always be among the very top ones, at least as far as the human species is concerned, even if we take into account the portentous future possibilities of nuclear war or rampant global warming.

Naturally, these ends of the world occasioned by the advance of the modernization front, which began precisely with the *plus ultra!* of European expansion in the sixteenth century, continue to take place at different scales, in several more or less remote parts of the planet, to this day. It is not necessary to insist on what goes on today in Africa, New Guinea, or the Amazon – or, to pick our examples from further up North, in those indigenous territories in the United States and Canada suffering the impacts of hydraulic fracturing or fracking. "Fracturing" is in fact a most appropriate word; for it is as if the end of the world were a truly *fractal event*, indefinitely reproduced at different scales, from ethnocidal wars in parts of Africa to the systematic assassination of indigenous leaders or environmental activists in the Amazon, from the purchase of vast portions of poor countries by hyperindustrial powers to the squatting and deforestation of indigenous land by mining and agribusiness, to the forcible exodus of peasant families only to give way to the expansion of transgenic soya...Not to mention the fractalization of the end that runs across the Great Chain of Being from top to bottom with the disappearance of countless *Umwelten* of living things.[53] Gaia is "just" the name of the *final* reckoning of these figures of the end; Gaia is, in short, the maximal scale that we can reach.

If the Humans who invaded it represented the indigenous America of the sixteenth and seventeenth centuries as a *world without humans* – be it because they objectively depopulated it, be it because the humans they found there did not fit the category of "Humans" – the surviving Indians, fully entitled Terrans from that New World, reciprocally found themselves as *humans without world*: castaways, refugees, precarious lodgers in a world in which they no longer belonged, because it could not belong to them. *And yet, it just so happens that many of them survived.* They carried on in *another world*, a world of others, their invaders and overlords. Some adapted and became "modernized," but in ways that bear little relation to what Moderns understand by that word. Others still struggle to hold on to whatever little world is left to them, and hope that, in the meantime, the Whites will not manage to destroy their own White world, now become for all living beings the "common world" – in a rather non-Latourian sense.

It strikes us as powerfully symbolic that one of the recent versions of the end of the world that captured the attention and excitement of this new generation of planetary gawkers that is the vast globalized audience of the Web, should be the so-called "Mayan Apocalypse" due to take place on December 21, 2012. As we can obviously notice, the world did not end, which was something that in any case had never been foretold by any written or oral Mayan indigenous tradition. The mistake notwithstanding, it is not unreasonable to connect the name of the Maya to the idea of the "end of the world," nor should we overlook the significance of the fact that the only date from a supposedly Amerindian calendar to be incorporated into world pop culture refers to an apocalypse.

As a matter of fact, Mayan history has known several "ends." First of all, the great Mesoamerican civilization that left us monuments such as Chichen Itzá, Tikal, and Copán went through a slow decadence between the seventh and tenth centuries, in all likelihood due to a combination of sociopolitical conflicts (revolts and wars) and prolonged environmental stress (droughts linked to El Niño events, depletion of cultivable soils), ultimately leading to the collapse of their society, the abandonment of those majestic pyramids and temples, and, very probably, of the scientific and artistic culture that flourished in those jungle cities. A first, pre-Columbian end of the world, then, which can serve us as example and warning regarding contemporary processes in which economy and ecology are entering collapse-inducing feedback loops at the same time as insurrectional events sprout here and there all over the planet.[54] Following that, with the invasion of the Americas in the sixteenth century, the Maya were, like the other native peoples of the continent, subjected and enslaved, as well as ravaged by epidemics brought by the invaders.[55] The genocide of Amerindian peoples – the end of the world for them – was the beginning of the modern world for Europe: without the despoiling of the Americas, Europe would have never become more than the backyard of Eurasia, the home continent of civilizations that were much richer than the Europeans during "our" Middle Ages (Byzantium, China, India, the Arab polities). No pillage of the Americas, no capitalism, no Industrial Revolution, thus perhaps no Anthropocene either. This second end of the world that hit the Maya is even more emblematic, if we consider that the first tirade against that genocide came from the bishop of Chiapas, Bartolomé de las Casas, a champion of human rights who early on regretted the brutal treatment dealt by the very Catholic Europeans to the Indians in his bishopric.

All that considered, even though they have gone through successive ends of the world, even though they have been reduced to a poor and oppressed peasantry, have had their territory broken up and handed over to different nation-states (Mexico, Guatemala, Belize, Honduras, El Salvador), the Maya continue to exist, their population grows, their world resists: diminished but defiant.

And it is indeed the Maya who offer us today what may be the best example of a "successful" popular insurrection against the two-headed State-Market monster that oppresses the world's minorities. (Namely, "successful" in that it did not eventually turn into something else.) The only revolt of an indigenous people in Latin America that managed to sustain itself without degenerating into a national state project; most importantly, the only one to have chosen its own cosmopolitical path, quickly abandoning the so-called "Marxist" revolutionary eschatology (profoundly Christian, in actual fact) with which Europe, through the mediation of its caste of clergymen/intellectuals, continues to try to control struggles for emancipation. We speak, of course, of the Zapatista uprising in Chiapas, that rare revolt that is a model of "sustainability" – political sustainability, also and above all. The Maya, who lived through their various ends of the world, show us today how it is possible to live after the end of the world. How, in short, it is possible to challenge the State and the Market, and to enact the right to self-determination.

Veritable end-of-the-world experts, the Maya and all other indigenous peoples of the Americas have a lot to teach us now that we are on the verge of a process in which the planet as a whole will become something like sixteenth-century America: a world invaded, wrecked, and razed by barbarian foreigners. Let the reader imagine herself watching – or rather, acting in – a sci-fi B movie in which the Earth is taken over by an alien race pretending to be humans, whose goal is to dominate the planet and to extract all its resources, after having used up their own home planet to the full. Usually, the aliens in such films feed on humans themselves: their blood, mental energy, and so forth. And now let the reader imagine that this *has already happened*, and that the alien race is, in fact, "*we ourselves.*" We were taken over by a species disguised as human, and they have won: we are they. Or are there in fact two different species of human, as Latour suggests – an indigenous and an alien one? Maybe it is the species as a whole and each one of us individually that is split in two, the alien and the indigenous living side by side in the same body: suppose a small shift in sensibility has suddenly made that self-colonization visible to us. We would thus all be indigenous, that is, Terrans, invaded by Europeans, that is, Humans; all of us, of course, including Europeans, who were after all the first Terrans to be invaded. A perfect intensive doubling (*plus intra!*), the end of extensive partitions: the invaders are the invaded, the colonized are the colonizers. We have woken up to an incomprehensible nightmare. And, as Oswald de Andrade put it, only the naked man shall understand.

Conclusion
World on the brink

Willing war against past and future wars, the pang of
deaths against all deaths, and the wound against all scars,
in the name of becoming and not of the eternal.

Deleuze and Guattari

We have discussed three thinkers that have guided us in a
good deal of our path up to this point, but we have failed
thus far to draw attention to a fourth and no less essential
one: Isabelle Stengers. For some years, at least since the
original publication of the French edition of *In Catastrophic
Times: Resisting the Coming Barbarism* in 2009, Stengers
has attempted to bring into play the complex and ambiguous
figure of Gaia, posited as key to understanding the "catastrophic times" that are ours. Stengers' Gaia is not, however,
the same entity as Latour's.[1] To begin with, she is the name
of an *event*, the face of the intrusion into our histories of a
kind of "transcendence" that we will never again be able
not to take into account: the cataclysmic horizon defined
by anthropogenic global warming. Gaia is the event that
places our world at risk, the only world that *we* have, *therefore*...(Stengers 2013b: 135). As we shall see, it is precisely
this "therefore" that marks the spot where it is necessary to
stop and think: to think about the consequences that one can
expect to draw from this "therefore," which are intimately

connected to the political extension that one chooses to give this "we."

Gaia is the transcendence that *responds*, in a brutally implacable way, to the equally indifferent transcendence, because brutally irresponsible, of Capitalism. If the Anthropocene, in the sense Chakrabarty and Latour ascribe to it, is the name of an *effect* that impacts all the inhabitants of the planet, Stengers' Gaia is the name of an *operation*,[2] that is, of the effect that this effect should have on those who caused it:

> Climate disorder, and the ensemble of other processes that poison life on Earth and have as their common origin what one [*on*] used to call development, certainly concern all who inhabit this Earth, from fish to men. But to name Gaia is an operation directed to "us" [Moderns], which seeks to elicit a "we" in the place of a "one" [*on*]. (Stengers 2013b: 115)

Stengers is drawing attention here to the Great Divide which has for the last centuries opposed those "peoples" who allegedly lived in an oneiric, phantasmatic relationship with the Earth, and a "we" that took itself for an impersonal "one," an abstract Third Person: the *anonymous* point of view from which "one" could apprehend nature's real essence, and of which we Moderns were the zealous guardians. "Gaia" therefore concerns "us" above all: "we" who believed ourselves to be shining beacons of humankind and who assigned ourselves the mission to civilize, modernize, and, naturally, render profitable the world's other peoples. Stengers seems to be saying, in a formula that combines Latour's terms and a crucial distinction proposed by Deleuze and Guattari: it is time to make Humans recognize that they are not responsible *for* Terrans, but *before* them. There is no possible negotiation without this recognition – no uncircumventable composition with Gaia if we do not convince ourselves first that there is no possible composition with the absolutely uncivilizable logic of capitalism.

More important perhaps than this first difference between Stengers' and Latour's respective understandings of Gaia is another one, suggested by the very subtitle of the former's 2009 book: the reminder that from now on we will always have to take Gaia into account is coupled with a call to *resist the coming barbarism*. This can be usefully contrasted with the Latourian idea that we are faced with a *war* that *could lead us to peace*. For Stengers, Gaia is not "what must unite all of the Earth's peoples" (2013b: 117); it is not a name that promotes unity and belonging, but an intrusion and a malaise. Gaia is a call to resist the Anthropocene, that is, to learn to live with(in) it and against it, which is also to say, *against ourselves*. The enemy, in short, is "us" – we Humans. As Latour had already remarked in his Gifford Lectures, the onset of the Anthropocene marks the end of the Human – as well as, and now it is Stengers (2013b: 125) who speaks, the obligation "to dream other dreams":

> As long as we are obsessed with the ideal model of a rational, objective knowledge capable of bringing all of the Earth's peoples into agreement with each other, regardless of whether it is in order to promote it or deconstruct it, we will remain incapable of establishing with these other peoples relations worthy of that name. (Stengers 2013b: 124)

We should note that, for Stengers, the concept of Gaia has proven itself an important antidote to the concept of the Anthropocene. She sides, in that position, with the likes of Donna Haraway and Elizabeth Povinelli, for whom the latter concept risks smuggling, under its merely denotative meaning of a geological epoch (whose threatening actuality none of them questions), a metaphysics that is anthropocentric (Haraway) or even unduly biocentric (Povinelli). That is, one that ascribes to *Homo sapiens* a "destinal" (even if only destructive) power over the planet's history in abstraction from the participations that implicate our species with numerous others, but which also develop elsewhere, in networks, places, scales, and dimensions very distant from our epistemological jurisdiction and our technological imagination. In this sense, Stenger's Gaia, Haraway's (2013) "staying with the trouble" and "becoming with," as well as Povinelli's (2013) "geontology" (which draws its inspiration from Australian aboriginal worlds), might be described as innovative transformations (double structural twists, as Lévi-Strauss would put it) of the mythical scheme of a "world without humans." Be that in the sense that the world is itself, as a multiverse traversed by multiple non-human ontologies, implicated in a becoming that demands that we learn how to follow it; be that in the sense that Humans must give way to those who Latour has called Terrans: all beings taken as parts of the world and as so many points of view the overlap of which *constitutes* the world – and which are as such (if it is at all possible to think them "as such") discordant monadological expressions of a World without antonym or antagonist, as it is not an Object waiting for a Subject to bestow it with synthetic unity from a transcendent perspective. The world "without Man" of this Anthropocene lived in the mode of resistance would thus converge with the world "made of people" of Amerindian cosmogonies: Gaia's definitive transcendence becomes indistinguishable from the originary anthropogeomorphic immanence postulated by the "people of Pachamama."

§ Pachamama, the "Mother of World-Time," is a deity that at least originally had no attributes that we would consider "characteristically maternal," as is in fact the case with all terrestrial deities of Andean and Mesoamerican cultures. After the Conquest, it was progressively domesticated through its association with the Virgin Mary; its image as "Good Mother Earth" is a New Age addition to the myth, which did not fail to stir some perplexity and/or metacultural adhesion (a "strategic Pachamamismo"?) among the indigenous of South America's plateaus. The notion's fate in the official political imaginary of Andean countries has been amply discussed of late. We refer the reader to Galinier and Molinié (2006), an exceedingly rich book ethnographically speaking, even if somewhat marred by a slightly grating "demystifying" impetus. Despite all the equivocations, however, one of the advantages of Pachamama over Gaia (although we acknowledge it is not enough to make us fight over it) is that it at least does not speak Greek. One more effort if we want to make room for others, after all...It is no doubt not merely a coincidence that all the vocabulary mobilized by the planet's present crisis comes (as do, in fact, the words "planet" and "crisis") from our ancient mythical language: Anthropocene, Gaia, catastrophe, cataclysm, apocalypse...(Bruno Latour probes deep here with his trinity of *demos*, *nomos*, and *theos*). We anticipate the day when global warming, having arrived at an incendiary +8°C, will be called *ekpyrosis* instead of the good old Latin equivalent, "conflagration."

In a way that is entirely alien to physicalist eliminativisms and "spiritualist" dualisms, but also – why not? – entirely alien to the so-called "correlationist" dialectic, the relation between humanity and world can begin to be thought as the relation connecting the one side of a Möbius strip to itself: as a non-orientable figure in which the inseparability of thought and being, animate and inanimate, culture and nature is not similar to the logical or formal inseparability of the verse and reverse of a same coin (what stuff would that coin be made of, by the bye?), but rather a complete and real consubstantiality or oneness, precisely like the surface of the Möbius strip.[3] Humanity and world are *literally* on the same side; the distinction between the two terms is arbitrary and impalpable: if one starts from humanity (thought, culture, language, the "inside") one necessarily arrives at the world (being, matter, nature, the "Great Outdoors") *without crossing any border* and conversely. "PLURALISM = MONISM," the magical formula sought by Deleuze and Guattari (1987: 20) can also be written, when read by a Tardean sorcerer or an Amerindian shaman, as "Pan-psychism = Materialism."[4]

Those who are on "the other side," that is, those who believe themselves to be *outside* the unbroken humanity-world surface, are those who see themselves imbued with the mission of severing this Möbius strip with the modernist scissors of "humankind's denaturalizing vocation" – these are the enemies. The problem, as we have seen, is that these enemies, at least as far as the good old ways of organizing the political spectrum are concerned, can be found to the left as well as to the right. Reciprocal accusations proliferate today – but, then again, that has always been the case – between those who picture themselves as heirs to the classic political dream that defined the left, namely the idea that "another world is possible." We shall not forgo the pleasure of playing that blame game here either. That the present essay intends first and foremost to be an initial description of what we see as the colossal effort of contemporary imagination to produce a thought and a mythology that are adequate to our times, does not prevent us – has not prevented us so far, as must be abundantly clear – from taking the side of some versions of this effort against others.

One of the most captivating debates taking place at the moment revolves around the speed of history and its variation. It opposes that philosophical (metaphysical, political, aesthetic) current that proposes a *political economy of acceleration* and the partisans of a *political ecology of deceleration*, of which Isabelle Stengers (2013b, 2015) has been an increasingly vocal supporter, and which unfolds into a set of themes which she shares with Bruno Latour: "hesitation," "attention," "diplomacy," and the need for "making room for others."[5]

In the aforementioned first "Accelerationist Manifesto," the authors make an observation that strikes us as most important:

> We believe the most important division in today's left is between those that hold to a folk politics of localism, direct action, and relentless horizontalism, and those that outline what must become called an accelerationist politics at ease with a modernity of abstraction, complexity, globality, and technology. (Williams and Srnicek 2013)[6]

As for us, we also take the diagnosis to be roughly accurate; that is indeed the most important fracture in the "left" today. To be sure, what we do not agree with *at all* is the obvious preference displayed in this paragraph, and developed throughout the "Manifesto," according to which the first option – what is dismissively described as "folk politics" – is retrograde and preservationist, whereas the second option would be the only one capable of leading us into the post-industrial Promised Land, where the spindles will not only work on their own but will apparently have no concrete "externalities" whatsoever either; our times are after all characterized by abstraction. Technology will provide.

As we have already said, it seems to us that it is precisely this "accelerationist politics," explicitly inspired by the Eurocentric eschatology of Progress, that is nostalgic of a rationalist, imperialist, triumphalist past – "what the left must reconnect to is its roots in the Enlightenment" (Srnicek, Williams, and Avanessian 2014) – and the persistence of its faith in the liberating virtues of automation and technical progress is only possible on the condition of a glaring blindspot bang in the middle of its futurological vision: the intrusion of Gaia, no less.

Both manifestos insist on the virtues of technological acceleration without saying a word about the material conditions

– energetic, environmental, geopolitical, etc. – required by
the process that would, if the authors are to be believed, lead
us "automatically" to the reduction of working hours (also
in Bangladesh? when?), the increase of leisure time (society
of the spectacle comes out of the closet!⁷), universal income,
and so forth.

> Against those across the political spectrum who indulge in the
> fantasy of local, small-scaled solutions to our many crises, this
> requires us to re-engineer our complex, abstract, and multi-
> scalar world without seeking to simplify it according to some
> pre-conceived schema. In place of folk political solutions, we
> should be pushing for full automation of work, reduction of
> the working week, and a universal basic income for everyone.
> (Srnicek, Williams, and Avanessian 2014)⁸

The *other* acceleration, the one that concerns the crossing
of critical thresholds in environmental parameters – *When*
will we get to +4°C, which may well become +6°C or +8°C?
When will fishing stocks run out? *When* will the Amazon
rainforest become an easily combustible savannah? *How*
many millions of climate refugees will try to break into Fortress Europe?⁹ – is given at most a nod bordering on frivolity,
not to say denialism pure and simple: "Today, it is *common
sense* to presume that climate change and its effects will
wreak havoc on the environment..." (Srnicek, Williams, and
Avanessian 2014; our emphasis).

As Stengers would say, "our dreams of liberation put us in
opposition to one another" (2013b: 124). Indeed...It cannot
but strike us as curious that accelerationists, whose alleged
main source of inspiration is a passage in *Anti-Oedipus* about
the need to push capitalism into an explosive tension in the
direction of ever more deterritorialization and a total decod-
ing of flows, have opted at the same time for an unequivocally
molar, majoritarian conception of politics, economy, and,
above all, of who the virtual addressees of their message are.
In general, their discourses do not mobilize any sociopolitical
category aside from "capitalism," "workers," "global civilization," "humankind," or "the masses." The existence and
resistance of other collectives outside the narcissistic circuit of
"Us" is ignored, or maybe filed under the equally broad category of "folk." Perhaps this is because, for accelerationists,

otherness has disappeared from the face of Earth, and these peoples no longer exist as poles of articulation of *other* "We"; or maybe because, in any case, what is left of them will perish in the flames of the redemptive conflagration that will launch "us" in the direction of the post-capitalist millennium. In their Ilumminati-like, vanguardist politics of "non-exclusive exclusion," they propose that the

> overwhelming privileging of democracy-as-process needs to be left behind. The fetishisation of openness, horizontality, and inclusion of much of today's "radical" left set the stage for ineffectiveness. Secrecy, verticality, and exclusion all have their place as well in effective political action (though not, of course, an exclusive one). (Williams and Srnicek 2013)[10]

The authors of the "Manifesto" thus not only pass over in silence those numerous subject-collectives that remain *other*, those peoples for whom universal real subsumption still has not transmuted into unconditional moral submission. Instead, they display a forgetfulness, which is ultimately perfectly humanist, of the numberless non-human entities, lineages, and societies that compose the planet. After all, are there accelerationist animals, apart maybe from those who await their hour in the abattoirs and milk or egg factories? We suspect not. On the other hand, we can all see the abundant existence in this vast world of "folk" machines, slow but very efficacious, which function in an entirely "local" way (even the celebrated "universal machine" must realize itself materially, therefore locally, in order to function). That they are not in any way sufficient to sustain current sociotechnical processes, there is no doubt. The question is whether they might not be, owing to imperatives of a different order – those that we find inscribed under the name of Gaia – ever more viable, ever more indispensable, ever more ahead of us instead of behind.[11]

Accelerationists, in short, wish to find a compromise with capitalism in the hope of transcending it – to be cleverer than it, so to speak – so as to escape its properly spiritual power of capture (sorcery, vampirism, zombiefication).[12] The problem, if we follow Stengers' line of argument, is that there is no sense in compromising with capitalism: there is only fighting it. Against Gaia, on the other hand – an indifferent material assemblage rather than a malign spiritual power – there is no sense in fighting, but only compromising, *composing with*, because its intrusive transcendence has from now on rendered ridiculous all epic or historical versions of human history, forcing us to *think* this situation, unheard of in modernity, which is *the absence of choice*:

> And perhaps the test will demand the abandoning, without any nostalgia, of the heritage of a nineteenth century dazzled by the progress of science and technology, cutting the link then established between emancipation and what I would call an "epic" version of materialism, a version that tends to substitute the tale of a conquest of nature by human labor for the fable of Man "created to have dominion over the earth." It is a seductive conceptual trick but one that bets on an earth available for this dominion or conquest. (Stengers 2015: 58)

The ever legitimate (how could it not be?) desideratum of "emancipation" must therefore be radically decoupled from the anthropological machismo implied in the idea of an epic conquest of nature and the meanings that the nineteenth century ascribed to the notion of "progress" – meanings that accelerationists, incorrigibly nostalgic as they are, hope to preserve. Thinking the world as transcendentally heterogeneous to Man, Moderns thought it as empirically "gratis," inexhaustible and infinitely available for appropriation. The material cost of freedom never crossed their minds; it was maybe enough to just chop off the heads of a few capitalists...As Chakrabarty (2009: 208) pointed out, however:

> In no discussion of freedom in the period since the Enlightenment was there ever any awareness of the geological agency that human beings were acquiring at the same time as and through processes closely linked to their acquisition of freedom. Philosophers of freedom were mainly, and understandably, concerned with how humans would escape the injustice, oppression, inequality, or even uniformity foisted on them by other humans or human-made systems. Geological time and the chronology of human histories remained unrelated. This distance between the two calendars, as we have seen, is what climate scientists now claim has collapsed. The period I have mentioned, from 1750 to now, is also the time

when human beings switched from wood and other renewable fuels to large-scale use of fossil fuel – first coal and then
oil and gas. The mansion of modern freedoms stands on an
ever-expanding base of fossil-fuel use. Most of our freedoms
so far have been energy-intensive.

This is why the name of Gaia is an *anti-modernist* prov-
ocation, a way of rendering explicit the "quasi-denialist"
(Stengers 2013a: 177) stance of the harbingers of "left accelerationism" – that is, of that position that Badiou curiously
dubbed "affirmationist," whose fear is that the intrusion of
Gaia will disturb the dream of perfect freedom, the freedom
resulting from the Promethean mastery that will lead to an
ontologically disembodied state, a techno-angelic transfiguration. We should maybe ask who it is that has been taking
opium lately.

Let us now briefly consider the question of urgency, or, to
put it differently, of the speed that imposes itself on present
action as seen under the light of what has happened in the
past. We mentioned above Stengers' hesitation in the face
of the consequences (*"therefore..."*) that one must draw
from the fact that Gaia is an urgent and global threat. She
believes that this sense of urgency can be easily converted
into a premature and authoritarian macropolitics of unification of the world and of *anthropos*. The possibility that
she fears is that the sciences in particular will be once again
mobilized to legitimize a kind of "war ecology," a state of
exception decreed by some supranational agency (under the
control of the geopolitical establishment, naturally), which
will hitch contemporary scientific research even more firmly
to the energy-devouring machine that moves the planetary
economy – beyond or behind the backs of, we should note,
the dreams of emancipatory universalization that the advent
of an "immaterial economy" would promote. The recourse to
urgency could just end up masking the prodigious flowering
of a satanic gospel of "development"; a development that
will of course now be green, sustainable, and intensive in
cognitive – and material, of course – capital.[13] This Market
would be supported by the decrees and armies of a world
State that would impose an even more absolute silencing of
those peoples, persons, and countries to suffer the "sad but

necessary consequences" of decisions taken in the name of urgency. Stengers (2013b: 139) warns: "It is evidently legitimate to experience a sense of urgency, but the danger is to leave aside, in the name of urgency, the question of what will happen when this urgency is finally recognized." This is why she insists so much, and not without reason, on a "cosmopolitical slowing down" of political process. This seems to us to be a correlate, and a no less imperative, urgent even, condition for a deceleration of the world economy – that is, a radical *redistribution* of the rates of "growth" legitimately or otherwise expected by various national economies – that would involve a profound reorientation of the model of technological evolution of "productive forces," and a broad dialogical opening which would entail a *literally* diplomatic conversation with the human and non-human populations that await the implacable consequences of the irresponsibility of Moderns. This cosmopolitical slowing down, says Stengers (2013b: 139; our emphasis), "pertains to the same world that invented politics as an exclusively human question" – which is not, as we have seen, the case of several other "human" worlds revealed by anthropology – and therefore "responds to a problem that is *ours*, and to the atrocious consequences that the intrusion of Gaia could elicit if that response takes place under the mode of urgency."

Let us recognize, at any rate, that Humans (in Latour's sense of the word) have already lost the war; *their world is already over*. Terrans, on the contrary, cannot lose the war, in both the imperative and the constative sense of "cannot." It remains to be seen how many humans (in Linnaeus' sense of the word) will be left in the Terran camp in the coming decades.

To believe in the world

A curiously recurrent topos in discourses on the environmental crisis – among those who ponder the alternatives for dealing with the catastrophe that is already here as much as among those (left and right) accelerationists who believe in an imminent rapture that will carry us into a new ontological stage, and finally also the partisans of business as usual and "drill, baby, drill" – is that "history does not move back-ward," that "we cannot go back to the Stone Age" (or the Middle Age, or the Garden of Eden...). Why do all sides seem to be in agreement on at least this point: "we cannot go back"? Considering that what is at issue here is obviously not the equally enticing physical question concerning the "arrow of time," and that it is perfectly evident that we cannot move backward *chronologically* – at least not accord-ing to our present ontological vulgate, which we see no reason to contest here – we should wonder what is so seem-ingly obvious about this oft-repeated sentence. What makes it so appealing or, rather, what makes doubting its pertinence so shocking?

We have two things to say about this before we draw to a close our exploration of present mythologies about the end of the world and of humanity. First of all, the incapacity to mourn that which is already dead is dreadful; worse still, it is deadly. Each day that goes by confirms the impression that we are already living, and shall live more and more, in a radically diminished world. As we said before, reducing the scale of our feats and ambitions will in all likelihood not just be a matter of choice.

Second, however, this does not mean that we are here simply to remark that the *world* has already ended, is ending, or will end soon. There are many worlds in the World.[14] We were saying above that we have a lot to learn from these minor peoples who resist in an impoverished world which is not even their own any more. Let us once again remember the fragility and transparence of the "magic cave" built by "Aunt Steelbreaker" in Lars Von Trier's *Melancholia*. Maybe nothing will ever look as pointless and pathetic as this purely formal shelter, a rough sketch of an indigenous teepee, and the small ritual that takes place inside it for a few seconds. Yet what takes place there, far from being a "merely" desperate and futile ritual, is a masterful bricolage, an *emergency solu-tion*, a wild concept-object that expresses an acute percep-tion of the essentially technical, technological nature of the efficacious ritual gesture. That little hut is the *only thing* in that moment that is capable of transforming the inescapable effect of the shock (Stenger's "*therefore...*") into an event, in the sense that Deleuze and Guattari (1994: 156) give to that concept when they say it is "the part that eludes its own actualization in everything that happens." There, in that almost purely virtual hut, inside and outside become indistinguishable, and past, present, and future coalesce, as in the time machine in H. G. Wells' homonymous book (yet another great myth about the worldless humans of the future). Or, rather, what passes (the *pass*) in that hut is an operation of deceleration, of slowing down, which enables the extraction of a paradoxical dimension of time, elicits a change in the order of sense, "such that time is interrupted in order to be resumed on another plane" (Zourabichvili 2012: 143). Dead time (Deleuze and Guattari 1994: 158), like that of *The Turin Horse*, in which nothing passes apart from the gypsies' cart, which in any case passes on a completely other plane, the plane of the event and of becoming ("Chrysippus taught: 'If you say something, it passes through your lips; so, if you say "chariot", a chariot passes through your lips.'" Deleuze 1990: 18).

Just as we once abhorred the vacuum, today we find repugnant the very idea of deceleration, regression, retreat, limitation, degrowth, applying brakes, descent – *sufficiency*.[15] Anything that brings to mind any of these movements toward an intensive sufficiency of world (instead of an epic overcoming of the "limits" separating us from a hyperworld) is immediately accused of naïve localism, primitivism, irrationalism, bad conscience, guilt, or even just fascistic tendencies, period.[16] In almost all the dominant forms of "our" historico-futurological imagination today, there is only one thinkable and desirable direction, the one that goes from "negative" to "positive": from less to more, from the possession of little to the property of much, from "techniques of subsistence" to "cutting-edge technology," from the Paleolithic nomad to the modern cosmopolitan citizen, from the savage Indian to the civilized worker (Danowski 2012b). This is why, when peasant communities "undergoing modernization" decide to *go back to being indigenous*, proving judicially their historical continuity with native peoples that are extinct as far as the official records are concerned, as so many groups in rural Brazil have done since the 1988 Constitution – which gave indigenous people and the descendants of slaves the right to collectively possess the land they and their ancestors have lived in – the furious, scandalized reaction of the dominant classes is such a spectacle to behold.

Unfortunately, one cannot laugh too long at those who still have their hand on the whip; the wrath and greed of those for whom the inexistence of otherness is an imperative has translated itself into a concerted offensive, through legal and illegal, legislative and criminal means, by big landowners (and their partners, clients, bosses) against Indians and other "traditional" peoples of Brazil.

Thus it is that it is only deemed possible (and desirable) for an individual or community to *stop being* indigenous, and impossible (and repulsive) to *go back to being* indigenous (Viveiros de Castro 2006). How can someone *desire back-wardness* as their *future*? Maybe the scandal has a reason for being: maybe it is impossible historically to go back to being indigenous. But it is perfectly possible – more than that, this is actually taking place – to experience a *becoming-indigenous*, local and global, particular as well as general; a *ceaseless rebecoming-indigenous* that has taken hold of sizeable sectors of the Brazilian population in an entirely unexpected way. This is one of the most important political *events* that we witness in Brazil today, which has progressively contaminated many Brazilian peoples other than the indigenous. Brazil is an enormous Aldeia Maracanã: here everyone is indigenous, except the ones who are not.[17] And we all know perfectly well who are those who are not, and where they are.[18]

It is in this sense then that Indians, the "people of Pachamama" to speak in Latour's gently ironic voice, are not the only Terrans, but no doubt have all the right to share that title. The autochtonous peoples of the American continent – the collectives of humans and non-humans whose history dates back to millennia before their collision with planet Commodity – are only a small part of contemporary Terran Resistance, this broad clandestine movement that has only begun to make itself visible in the planet occupied by the Moderns: in Africa, Australasia, Mongolia, in the backstreets and basements of Fortress Europe. They are not really in a position to lead any final combats or cosmopolitical Arma-geddons; it would be ridiculous to picture them as the seed of a new Majority. Above all, we should not expect that, if they could, they would run to the rescue of Humans, to redeem or justify those who have persecuted them implacably for five centuries. Tired of a long history of systematic treachery, it would be no surprise if they were not interested in "negotiating" any cosmopolitical peace, and deservedly let us burn in hell. In any case, apart from the fact that they still are a crucial component of the demotic megaculture of the three Americas (and the world at large), and as such capable of originating powerful and unexpected lines of flight of global impact, one thing is certain: Amerindian collectives, with their comparatively modest populations, their relatively simple technologies that are nonetheless open to high-intensity syncretic assemblages, are a "figuration of the future" (Krøijer 2010), *not a remnant of the past*. Masters of technoprimitivist bricolage and politico-metaphysical metamorphosis, they are one of the possible chances, in fact, of a *subsistence of the future*.[19]

To speak of the end of the world is to speak of the need to imagine, rather than a new world to replace our present one, a new people, *the people that is missing*. A people who believes in the world that it will have to create with whatever world we will have left them. So let us conclude with Gilles Deleuze (1995: 176), the younger brother of Oswald de Andrade:

> What we most lack is a belief in the world, we've quite lost the world, it's been taken from us. If you believe in the world you precipitate events, however inconspicuous, that elude control, you engender new space-times, however small their surface or volume.... Our ability to resist control, or our submission to it, has to be assessed at the level of our every move. We need both creativity *and* a people. (1995: 176)

Rio de Janeiro, July 2014

Notes

Prefatory note

1 Translator's note: a literal translation would be *Is There a World to Come? An Essay on Fears and Ends.*
2 We must not leave unmentioned two studies which appeared just as we finished this preface and which had a big impact on the public as well as on the scientific community: Richard E. Zeebe, Andy Ridgwell, and James C. Zachos (2016), and Hansen et al. (2016).

Chapter 1 What rough beast...

1 See, for instance, the latest reports produced by the Intergovernmental Panel on Climate Change (IPCC), which came to light in 2013–14 and can be found at <http://www.ipcc.ch>. As is well known, the IPCC's projections tend to figure among the most moderate among those circulating in the scientific community with regard to the speed and intensity of climate change.
2 On apocalyptic cinematography, the reader could do no better than consult Peter Szendy's (2015) *Apocalypse Cinema*, which comments on thirteen end-of-the-world films and includes instructive references to dozens of others. For an analysis of the proliferation of apocalyptic discourse in the curious cases

of dystopian fantasies directed at a female adolescent public, see Craig (2012).

3 The question regarding the pertinence of the concepts of human species ("humankind") and/or "humanity" as a way to frame the reflection and action of currently existing political collectivities in the face of environmental crisis (states, peoples, parties, social movements) will be taken up again in the conclusion of this essay.

4 The "Earth System" is a technical concept currently used by climatologists and other Earth scientists to refer to the geophysical cum macro-ecological parameters that characterize our planet.

5 Geological epoch of the Quaternary period that followed the Pleistocene at approximately 11,700 years before the year AD 2000 and continues into the present (until, that is, the "golden spike" marking the start of the Anthropocene has been agreed on – assuming it will be agreed on – by the geological community).

6 To end the world "in their own way," that is, by demolishing the concepts of world elaborated by modern philosophy, from Kant to Derrida and beyond (see Gaston 2013).

7 "A nuclear war would have been a conscious decision on the part of the powers that be. Climate change is an unintended consequence of human actions and shows, only through scientific analysis, the effects of our actions as a species" (Chakrabarty 2009: 221).

8 See Cook (2013a, 2013b). A comment on one of these posts points out that John Lyman (University of Hawaii) had already employed the comparison to the Hiroshima bomb in relation to ocean temperature in interviews about a study published in *Nature* (see Lyman et al. 2010; Israel 2010).

9 In the conclusion we shall see some of the reasons for the dissensus surrounding this concept as a way of naming the time in which we live and the event that befalls us.

10 On the "double twist" as the formula of structuralist transformation par excellence, see Maranda (2001); Almeida (2008); Viveiros de Castro (2014).

11 Eduardo Sterzi has done some important research on the theme of the wasteland, from its European origins to contemporary Brazilian literature. See, for instance, Sterzi (2009).

Chapter 2 ...Its hour come round at last...

1 And that knowledge, precisely, never stops surprising us. See, for example, the case studies on the accelerated melting of giant

glaciers in Greenland and the Antarctic, which only came to light weeks after the publication of the last part of the IPCC's latest report in April 2014.

2 Anders (2007: 82) observed this passage from condition to conditioned in regard to what he called "the time of the end" (*Endzeit*), the post-nuclear *kairós* defined by the imminent possibility of the "end of times" (*Zeitenende*). Translator's note: as Günther Anders' *Endzeit und Zeitenende* has not been translated into English, I have used the French edition consulted by the authors throughout. I have chosen to translate *Endzeit* as "time of the end" rather than the more idiomatic "end time" so as not only to fully differentiate it from "end of times" (since "end time" and "end of times" are often treated as synonymous in English), but also to retain the inverse symmetry that exists between the two terms (*Endzeit, Zeitenende*) in the original.

3 The authors have since published a revised, updated version of their study. See Steffen et al. (2015).

4 See Abraham (2014); Chery (2014); Freedman (2014).

5 It might be instructive to compare these considerations with the "ecopragmatist" argument of the notorious Breakthrough Institute (about which we shall have more to say later on) on the inadequacy of applying the notion of planetary limits on a *global* scale, which could block "opportunities" for growth at the *local* level; according to the latter, only climate change and the acidification of the oceans would really constitute subsystems with planetary limits. See Nordhaus, Shellenberger, and Blomqvist (2012: 6–15).

6 Translator's note: the Socio-Enviromental Institute (ISA) is a Brazilian NGO founded in 1994 whose work focuses on the defense of social and collective goods and rights, particularly the environment, and the rights of indigenous peoples. Eduardo Viveiros de Castro is one of its founding members, alongside several other important Brazilian anthropologists.

7 The hockey-stick graph, conceived by Michael Mann as a way of representing the changes in the Earth's temperature since 1000 CE (Current Era), made its first appearance in the "Summary for Policy Makers" section of the third IPCC report in 2001. For a review of the debate that it sparked, see Mann (2012).

8 These measures have been extended into farther periods in the past based on empirical observations (ice cores, tree rings, fossil records, etc.), some going back to 1100 BP as in the case of the "temperature anomaly." The growth of chronological coverage has reinforced the exceptionality of the present moment in what concerns the environment in which the human species developed.

9 The Keeling curve is one of the few graphs to present no negative oscillations apart from diuturnal and seasonal ones. Global temperatures, on the other hand, while displaying a clear rising tendency over extended periods, above all in the hockey-stick graphs including temperatures prior to the Industrial Revolution, often present punctual dips over shorter intervals of time. Any eventual *slower* rise in global temperature is of course readily celebrated by climate denialists as proof of the falsity of the "warming hypothesis," but can be easily explained by climatologists as taking place in connection with a more accentuated rise in other parameters; for instance, of deep-ocean temperature.

10 A study has attributed this phenomenon to the large floods that took place in Australia in the same period, which "took huge quantities of water out of the oceans without returning it, like a library user with mounting late fees" (Freedman 2013). See also Fasullo et al. (2013).

11 See Hansen et al. (2012).

12 See Wallace Broecker and Robert Kunzig, quoted in Chakrabarty (2014: 6): "Every now and then... nature has decided to give a good swift kick to the climate beast. And the beast has responded, as beasts will – violently and a little unpredictably."

13 Translator's note: although neither "ambiented" [*ambientado*] nor "ambienting" [*ambientante*] exist in English, I imagine the meaning of the wordplay in this passage will be clear to the reader. It should be noted that, although "*ambientante*" does not exist in Portuguese either, "*ambientado*" is common currency, usually used in the sense of "situated" or "set" (as in the sentence, "a story set in the 1950s"); whereas the root word, "*ambiente*," either in that form or as an adjective in "*meio ambiente*" [ambient medium or milieu], is the word for "environment," from which variations such as "environmental" [*ambiental*] and "environmentalist" [*ambientalista*] are equally derived.

14 See the chapter "10,000 B.C: The Geology of Morals (Who Does the Earth Think It Is?)" in *A Thousand Plateaus* (Deleuze and Guattari 1987), the date in whose title clearly refers to the Neolithic Revolution and the beginning of the Holocene.

15 See Brooke's (2014) monumental synthesis.

16 According to Pálsson et al. (2013: 4), the term "Anthropozoid" had already been suggested in 1873 by Italian geologist (and Catholic priest) Antonio Stoppani.

17 Now that we know we are not only a mortal but also mortiferous species, we should do something about it, as Monbiot (2014) suggests in relation to the recent literature on the extinction of the Pleistocene's megafauna.

18 See the network's Facebook page at: <https://www.facebook.com/
pages/World-Ecology-Research-Network/174713375900335>.

19 It is unknown to us whether Chakrabarty had Moore's acerbic
criticism specifically in mind here.

20 See also Anders' (2007: 40–51) trenchant pages on the "paralo-
gism of sensation": the personal indifference in the face of
the apocalypse owing to the fact that, as "everyone will die
together," it does not concern *me* as such.

21 On the acceleration of time, see Derrida's (1984) dense article,
which we have not had – *et pour cause* – the time to ruminate
adequately. See also Gaston (2013) for an exposition of the
Derridean critique of the metaphysical concept of "world" and
its correlates, as well as a defense of the philosopher against
the criticisms made by those that Gaston (Ibid.: 151ff) calls
"eco-polemicists."

22 See Anders (2007: 18–27) on the "*kairos* of ontology," a
moment created by the threat of apocalypse, and thus the end
of the age of "non-Being-for-us" and the advent of "non-Being-
for-no-one," the "true non-Being" of the extinction that will
abolish – that has always already abolished – the past as such.
This connection between what, half a century after Anders'
reflections, has come to be dubbed "the ontological turn" and
the perspective of the end of the world seems to us to be
fundamental.

23 The concept is taken up again in Deleuze and Guattari (1994:
16). Once again, see Gaston (2013: 99ff) for an analysis of
Derrida's statement that the death of the Other is the end of
the world.

24 "It must be remembered that the phrase 'actual world' is like
'yesterday' or 'tomorrow', in that it alters its meaning according
to standpoint" (Whitehead 1979: 65).

25 For the distinction between the "relativist" concept of world-
for-a-subject and the "perspectivist" concept of world-of-a-
subject, see Viveiros de Castro (2012a).

26 On this difference in the way of determining the conditions
of articulation of a "we," see the commentary on a phrase by
Richard Rorty in Viveiros de Castro (2011a).

27 Given the political intention of the present essay, it will not
surprise the reader that we consider more interesting ("better
to think with," as Lévi-Strauss might say) the people-without-
world variants than the world-without-people cases, and that it
is on those, therefore, that we should linger the most.

28 We will not discuss the technical nuances involved in the various
concepts of world historically developed "within" philosophy as
a discipline. For a partial analysis of that history, centered on

the Kant-Hegel-Husserl-Heidegger-Derrida series, we refer the reader again to Gaston's (2013) useful book.

29 The formula "the end of x as we know it" (where "x" could stand for the world, human life, civilization, the nation state etc.) is ever more ubiquitous in contemporary discourse and would merit a detailed analysis, as it is rich in philosophical understatements and assumptions underneath its ostensive idiomatic innocence: who, after all, is *"we"*?

Chapter 3 ...Slouches toward Bethlehem to be born?

1 See Danowski (2011a) for one of the texts that inspired this book, which proposes to read the recurrent use of certain fictitious situations in the work of David Hume (the reference to Adam among them) as configuring a kind of thought experiment on the possible meaning of a human nature "before" or "after" the world (understood here not as totality, but as "experience" which, in the case of these fictions, either did not yet exist or existed no longer).

2 Although it is hard to find environmental movements today that would demand the expulsion of traditional populations from their land in the name of the preservation of ecosystems, international initiatives such as REDD (Reducing Emissions from Deforestation and Forest Degradation) and REDD+ (where the "plus" emphasizes the aspect of conservation, sustainable management and the enhancement of carbon stock in forests above and beyond avoiding deforestation and recovering existing forests), often financed by the World Bank and other such development banks, have been severely criticized for having precisely that effect in the end. See, for example, No REDD in Africa Network (2014).

3 "I think, in the twentieth century, when our population quadrupled, we got to the point where we kind of redefined original sin. Just by being born, we're part of the problem." (Weisman 2013).

4 See, for instance, *Aftermath: Population Zero* (2008). One should not, however, confuse the book *The World Without Us* with the film *The World Without US* (as in the United States of America), a docufiction by Mitch Anderson and Jason Tomaric, also released in 2008.

5 The protagonist eventually comes across a handful of other survivors and leads an ultimately failed effort to rebuild civilization.

In his old age, finding himself forced to abandon this dream, he finally accepts the regression of his descendants and other humans into a state of cultural primitiveness as a hopeful new beginning.

6 In a subsequent interview, he seems to some extent to minimize the effects of climate change as having "happened a lot in the past" and as being susceptible to rapid absorption by the Earth's biosphere once humans disappear (Weisman 2009). It should be noted that the author's point of view here is, once again, that of life's resilience, not human survival.

7 For more information on the Voluntary Human Extinction Movement, see their self-presentation at <http://www.vhemt.org/aboutvhemt.htm>. Weisman, in the interview cited in the previous footnote, also evokes an imaginary interruption of human procreation as a "non-violent" way of recovering the *statu quo ante*.

Chapter 4 The outside without thought, or the death of the Other

1 We should recall here Michel Foucault's (1973) definition of this Man of the modern *episteme* as an "empirico-transcendental doublet."

2 See Coccia (2013) on "wordless philosophers," that is, the forsaking of philosophy of nature by epistemological humanism and historicism.

3 As a label, the term "speculative realism" enjoys greater currency in the Anglo-Saxon world; apart from Meillassoux, who participated in the original conference from which the "movement" took its name, French philosophers generally tend to be "coopted," if not against their will, at least *in absentia*. The last three in the above list have in fact been translated and abundantly commented upon by Brassier, Harman and other Anglophone speculative realists.

4 Shaviro (2011) has provided what is, to our minds, one of the clearest presentations of the ground that is common to the main figures of speculative realism, as well as some of the lines along which they part ways. See also the anthology organized by Bryant, Srnicek, and Harman (2011).

5 Or speculative materialism; the -ism may vary, the adjective remains constant.

6 The relative "simplicity" of this scientifically grounded imagining of the physical extinction of the human species as explored

by Weisman does not, we believe, detract from its determinant character in motivating contemporary metaphysical disquiet.

7 *"Le grand dehors"* ("the great outdoors") are common-use clichés in French and English to designate "nature," "wilderness," "wild life," the world that exists far from human agglomerations and madding crowds. Meillassoux employs it in an almost tongue-in-cheek way to refer to thought-independent reality or "uncorrelated" Being. The choice of words also includes a likely (and very likely ironic) allusion to the *dehors* of Blanchot, Foucault and other key thinkers in French poststructuralism.

8 "We are materialists in so far as we obey the two principles that belong to any materialism: being is not thought, and thought can think being" (Meillassoux 2012). Such a statement does not address the (materialist) question of the real being of thought: the fact that, even if being is not ("just") thought, thought is or has ("some") being. Thought, in its ontic dimension of a phenomenon that is internal to the world and therefore ontologically external to itself – which, among many other things, is a condition for the relevance of anthropology as an empirical discipline – is something that doesn't seem to concern the author. See in this regard, Markus Gabriel's (2009: 81–8) critique.

9 "I call 'hyperphysics' every theory that postulates a reality other than that investigated by science, qua heuristic explanation for the supposedly ultimate components of our world, itself recognized as one contingent world among others that are really possible" (Meillassoux 2012). Under this label, the author lumps together all vitalist and/or pan-experiantialist metaphysics, such as James's, Whitehead's, Bergson's, and Deleuze's.

10 See Nunes (2014), Gabriel (2009: 81–8).

11 This is tied in with a complex argument on the necessary absolute contingency of the cosmic order, the themes of "Hyperchaos" and "divine inexistence," which we cannot go into here. They include, among their consequences, the possibility of God coming to exist at any moment in the future.

12 We follow here Paul Ennis' (2013) lucid exposition as well as the aforementioned Shaviro (2011).

13 Whitehead's denunciation of the bifurcation of nature into primary and secondary qualities is repeatedly recalled by Latour, Shaviro and other "hyperphysicists" *sensu* Meillassoux.

14 For example, the profound melancholia of Justine, the protagonist; her ecstatic (reconciling?) bathing in the cold light of Melancholia; the telescope and the rudimentary gauge contrived by her brother-in-law (John), which allows her nephew (Leo) and then her sister (Claire) to see the planet's approximation; the

fragile teepee built to protect not only Leo, but also Claire and even Justine herself; and finally, of course, the "immediating" clash with Melancholia.

15 As the first part of the film makes clear, there is no way out from inside capitalism (see Shaviro 2012). There's something here that is reminiscent of Luís Buñuel's *The Exterminating Angel*, where a coterie of well-off bourgeois find themselves equally enclosed in a luxurious place that they cannot leave, for reasons as inexplicable as in von Trier's film.

16 The teepee is like the ones built by indigenous people of the North American prairies, but reduced to its skeletal structure, without anything to cover it.

17 See also the intriguing analysis of the film proposed by Marie Gil and Patrice Maniglier (2015), which, among other things, opens a whole new possibility of interpretation concerning the film's focal object, the magical teepee "inside" of which the characters receive the impact of the Event.

18 The expression is Brassier's, who uses it in a different context, primarily in reference to Freud's hypothesis of the death drive.

19 In this context, see Shaviro's (2011) reference to the works of Eugene Thacker, in which the latter distinguishes between a "world-for-us," a "world-in-itself," and a "world-without-us."

Chapter 5 Alone at last

1 As Bonneuil and Fressoz (2016) have rightly observed, awareness of the anthropic deterioration of the planet did not come all of a sudden, nor does it characterize the passage from an age of blindness and naiveté to the advent of a "reflexive modernity" in what regards ecological questions. It seems undeniable to us, however, that the accumulation of such anthropic modifications of the Earth's thermodynamic equilibrium became phenomenologically – or rather catastrophically – palpable only in the last decades of the twentieth century.

2 Although the whole action seems to unfold in the course of a single day, we are left in the dark as to what the date is.

3 See, for example, *Ubik, Do Androids Dream of Electric Sheep?, Flow My Tears (the Policeman Said)*, and *Counter-Clock World*.

4 Leibniz (1990: § 416). See Danowski (2011b) for an approach to Leibniz's optimism under the light of the present crisis. On human capacity to live in indefinitely worsening conditions, see

Hunt and Lipo's (2011) interesting (and depressing) hypothesis about Easter Island, as well as the lessons drawn by MacKinnon (2013); also Krulwich (2013).

5 On *The Matrix* as an "intellectual action movie" (as per the Wachowski brothers' self-description), see Badiou et al. (2003).

6 Maybe "we have already been dead" since the Eco 92 conference in Rio de Janeiro, June 1992. At least this is how Dick's *Ubik*, published in 1969, begins: "At three-thirty A.M. on the night of June 5, 1992, the top telepath in the Sol system fell off the map in the offices of Runciter Associates in New York City." June 5 was declared World Environment Day by the United Nations' General Assembly in 1972.

7 On Amerindian perspectivism, see Viveiros de Castro (2004). On the possibility of a point of view of the dead, see the words of Elizabeth Costello, the protagonist of J. M. Coetzee's (1999: 69) *The Lives of Animals*: " 'For instants at a time…I know what it is like to be a corpse…All of us have such moments, particularly as we grow older. The knowledge we have is not abstract…but embodied. For a moment we *are* that knowledge. We live the impossible: we live beyond our death, look back on it, yet look back as only a dead self can.' "

8 Another science-fiction classic that comes to mind here is Octavia Butler's (2005) "Speech sounds," which takes place in a world (a city) in which humans have lost the faculty of language owing to a mysterious disease, becoming murderous beasts that wander around in a crumbling material world.

9 The "action" in *The Turin Horse* takes place over the course of exactly seven days, enacting a veritable de-creation of the world: a Genesis narrated backwards, the inversion of a spectacular beginning.

10 See Kurzweil's (2005) book-length manifesto, as well as his succinct exposition in Kurzweil (2009), and Farman (2012) on "re-enchantment cosmologies." To have an idea of how those themes have been popularized, see Sonny (2013). The techno-theological mythology professed by Kurzweil and his fellow travelers (Vernon Vinge, Hans Moravec, William Bainbridge, Frank Tipler, John Barrow, and other "transhumanist" scientists) is only the most recent, some would say the most delirious, version the old project of cosmic colonialism, which is far from having been abandoned altogether (see Szendy 2011; Valentine 2012; Williams and Srnicek 2013): the extraplanetary expansion of the human species that would make it independent from any world in particular.

11 See Farman (2012) on the "intelligent cosmos" and human obsolescence.

12 The Singularity theme – "West Coast futurism," according to Farman (2012) – is associated to the high-tech culture of Silicon Valley. Kurzweil is today the Director of Engineering at Google.

13 Then again, maybe not all that hard. It is from a Breakthrough Institute paper that we have extracted the statement on "liberty and security" as capitalism's greatest achievements; and the presence among their senior fellows of Pascal Bruckner, an old *nouveau philosophe* rightwinger and self-professed enemy of "third-worldism" and "multiculturalism," as well as author of a recent diatribe against the "propaganda of fear" (see Bruckner 2014), strikes us as more than circumstantial evidence of the institute's penchants.

14 The institute's founders would rather define themselves as "modernists" or "ecopragmatists" or ferociously anti-environmental "ecologists." *Time* magazine, on the other hand, has defined them as "heroes of the environment"; see Walsh (2008). In its second, 2009 edition, the book's title was changed to *Break Through: Why We Can't Leave Saving the Planet to Environmentalists*. This is the edition that we will refer to throughout.

15 As Stengers opportunely reminds us, however, the Trojan Cassandra was right.

16 Translator's note: "we must let the cake rise before we share it" is a much-cited (and much-maligned) statement by Brazilian economist Delfim Netto, one of the key formulators of the economic policy of the country's military regime in the 1970s.

17 Bruno Latour has more than once expressed some sympathy towards the imaginary proposed by the Breakthrough Institute; see Latour (2011a) and the criticism directed at him by Hamilton (2012). In more recent times, however, Gaia's gravitational pull (in other words: a more realistic appraisal of the timeframe in which the environmental crisis unfolds) has made him revise this position, we dare say, dramatically. As for Clive Hamilton, his opposition to the prophets of the "good Anthropocene" has only grown stronger (Hamilton 2014).

18 On "second" and "first nature," see Latour (2013d).

19 See Lindblom (2012) on Nick Land's "vision" and his theory of a "meltdown" in the apocalyptic-Singularitarian mold.

20 Thus 1977, a dramatic year for Italian *Autonomia* and the darkest hour of what became known as the "years of lead"; Franco "Bifo" Berardi (2009) has pinpointed it as signaling both the "end of the [twentieth] century" and a "turning point in modernity." Among other major achievements listed by Berardi, this *annus horribilis* saw the foundation of Apple Computers, the death of Charles Chaplin and Johnny Rotten and Sid Vicious's "no future."

21 For more on ZAD, see the movement's website at: <http://zad.nadir.org>.

22 With its constant references to "maximal mastery," a future that must be "cracked open," a "hard-edged anti-humanism" and so forth, the rhetoric of the "Manifesto" suggests an oddly adolescent, hyper-masculine phallocentrism. On this point, see also Ordnung (2013). It is hard not to concede Isabelle Stengers' point when she reacts to a question on whether she has "concerns about the ethical tropes of political, aesthetic, or ontological accelerationism" and how she would define her own cosmopolitical position in contrast to accelerationism's "nihilistic heroism and its neglect of its own privilege" with the trenchant answer: "I decline contrasting *Cosmopolitics*, whatever its shortcomings, with that trash – they are male chauvinist pigs, that's all. I am only sorry for the memory of Félix Guattari, which they deface" (Stengers 2013a: 179).

23 Apparently, "we environmentalists" are forever condemned to either excess or lack of imagination. See, for example, Brazilian president Dilma Rousseff's declaration right before the Rio+20 Conference in 2012, in which she criticized activists opposing the damming of Amazonian rivers for the purpose of building giant hydroelectric power stations: "Nobody in a conference like this, I'm sorry, can agree to discuss fantasies. There is no room for fantasy here. I'm not talking about utopia, there is room for that; I'm talking about fantasy" (Domingos and Moura 2012). A year later, in May 2013, Dilma Rousseff's then chief of staff, Gleisi Hoffman, described the arguments of those who defend the constitutional right of indigenous people to their land as "unrealistic ideological projects" (CEPAT 2012).

24 Badiou perhaps had in mind this sentence by Sloterdijk (which is in fact one of the epigraphs in Latour's Gifford Lectures): "It is no longer politics pure and simple, but climate politics, which is our destiny" (2014: 537). The fact that Badiou chooses the idiosyncratic Sloterdijk as "the" philosopher of ecology strikes us as a case of Freudian displacement (where we read "Sloterdijk," we should maybe read "Serres," or "Guattari," or "Latour," or "Stengers"...), if not pure ignorance of what takes place outside his immediate intellectual world.

25 As in Saint Thomas Aquinas' heaven, there are no animals in the desert of the real described in Philip K. Dick's *Do Androids Dream of Electric Sheep?*, or in the land of the dead of the Wari', a people from the Western Amazon (Conklin 2001), let alone in the post-capitalist world. (In the case of the Wari', this is because the dead themselves are animals in the prey position – peccaries, which are the typical, preferred form of meat/food. Other dead,

belonging to other people, will for example be jaguars, occupying the opposite, predator or cannibal, pole of animality.) See
also Anders (2007: 75), who retreads in this passage an old
humanist cliché: "If the pre-human region whence we came is
that of *total animality*, the post-human region we are on the
verge of reaching is that of *total instrumentality*. The human
seems to stand out as an *intermezzo* between these two phases
of humanity (which resemble each other at least in what regards
their negative aspect)."

26 Oreskes and Conway (2014) have attempted a similar thought
experiment, although without Tarde's metaphysical resonances,
in a recent essay that takes *our* present future of climate catastrophe as its starting point.

27 The reader should bear in mind that Jules Verne's *Journey to the
Center of the Earth* was published in 1864, whilst Tarde began
work on the *Fragment* in 1879.

28 The ironic allusion to the allegory of the cave becomes virtually transparent in the following passage: "There is not, I have
already said, a city, but there is a grotto of philosophers, a
natural one to which they come, and sit apart from one another
or in groups, according to their schools, on chairs formed of
granite blocks beside a petrifying well. This spacious grotto
contains astounding stalactites, the slow product of continuous
droppings which vaguely imitate, in the eyes of those who are
not too critical, all kinds of beautiful objects... Such is the ample
cave which is exactly identical to the philosophy it shelters"
(Tarde 1974: 173–4).

29 The passage evokes several figures from Latour's pen, such as
the supralunar/sublunar opposition underlying the concept of
"Terran" as designating the people of Gaia, earthbound and
at war with the heaven-oriented Humans/Moderns (Latour
2013a); and the contrast between Science's discourse on the
"remote" [*lointain*] and Religion's access to the "nearby" [*prochain*]: "[I]t is when we speak of Science that we should raise
our eyes to the heavens, and when we speak of Religion that we
should lower them toward the Earth....When will we [Terrans]
come back to Earth?" (Latour 2013d: 322–4; modified to substitute "Terran" for "Earthling"). Translator's note: Latour is
playing here on a double meaning of "*prochain*" that works in
most Latin languages, but is impossible to convey in English;
the word can also be translated as "neighbor," as in the phrase
"love thy neighbor."

30 "[The disaster] has produced, so to say, a purification of society."
(Tarde 1974: 111).

31 As in every narrative in which humankind confronts a loss or lack of world, recourse to cannibalism insinuates itself every now and then; see, for instance, pp. 82, 55, 157.

32 It would be interesting to compare the monotony of Tarde's perfect society of pure humans without Nature to the monotony of the perfect world of pure souls without bodies considered, in response to Pierre Bayle's suggestion, by Leibniz (1990: §200) in the *Theodicy*. Contrary to what Bayle imagined, says Leibniz, a world composed of angels or gods only (a metaphysical impossibility, in fact) would be less perfect – and far more boring – than ours: without diversity in its essences, without contrast in its qualities, with nothing to be said or done; a world, in short, abstract and unreal. See Danowski (2001: 67–9).

33 Troglodytic love was strongly sublimated and reproductively sterile, birth control strict and meritocratic.

34 It is also worth comparing this "fragment of future history" with Günther Anders *Endzeit und Zeitenende*, which we could call a "Fragment on the Non-future of History"; see for example the sarcastic passages in Anders (2007: 22–3).

Chapter 6 A world of people

1 Tarde seems veritably obsessed with the Chinese, and displays an odd penchant for imagining them as pure sensible objects. We have already seen his use of this people as the paradigm for the color yellow; we could equally recall the disconcerting paragraph on the average height of China in *Monadology and Sociology*.

2 In the overwhelming majority of Amerindian languages (at least in Lowland South America), there is a single word that can be translated either as "human," "people," or "person," and which frequently, plays a pronominal ("we") rather than substantive syntactical or pragmatic role.

3 With some improvement in the moral field – literal cannibalism, for instance, becomes objectively unnecessary (although, in a few cases, it remained subjectively, that is, socially, imperative), since, with the advent of the cosmological era, animals and plants adequate to human nourishment appear.

4 "Many, if not all categories" – compare this to the Aikewara exception concerning tortoises in the characterization of the pan-human state of pre-cosmological reality. These provisos are important because they highlight an essential dimension of Amerindian mythocosmologies: such expressions as "nothing,"

"everything" or "all" function as qualifiers (not to say "qua-sifiers") more than as quantifiers. We cannot delve deeper into this discussion here, but it carries obvious implications as to the adequate comprehension of the indigenous concepts of "cosmos" and "reality." Everything, including *the* Everything, is only imperfectly totalizable: the exception, the remainder and the lacuna are (almost always...) the rule.

5 That statement would require some nuancing and differentiating in regard to several Amerindian cosmologies, not to mention the occasional exception to it. There is an ongoing debate on the extension and comprehension of this mythophilosopheme regarding a primordial or infrastructural humankind in indig-enous America, a debate that is tied with another one around the concepts of "animism" and "perspectivism," which we will not explore here.

6 Once more, see Anders (2007: 75): "the pre-human region whence we came is that of *total animality*."

7 "Ethnographic present" is the way anthropologists call – now-adays almost always with a critical intention, notwithstand-ing Hastrup's (1990) important defense of the notion – the discipline's classic narrative style, which situates monographic descriptions in a timeless present more or less coetaneous with the observer's fieldwork, or which "pretends" to ignore the "historical changes" (colonialism, etc.) that allowed, precisely, for ethnographic observation. We shall, however, use the expres-sion in a sense that is doubly opposed to that one, as a way to designate the attitude of "societies against the state" in regard to historicity. *Ethnographic present* is thus the time of Lévi-Strauss' "cold societies" – "societies against accelerationism" or *slow societies* (as one speaks of *slow food* or *slow science* – see Stengers 2013b), for whom all cosmopolitical changes necessary for human existence *have already taken place*, and the ethnos' task is to secure and reproduce this "always already."

8 An Amazonian metaphysician might call this the argument of "human ancestrality" or "the evidence of the anthropofossil".

9 Those beings in indigenous cosmologies that we classify under the heteroclitic category of "spirits" generally tend to be enti-ties that have preserved the ontological lability of the originary people, and which for that reason characteristically oscillate between human and animal, vegetable etc. determinations.

10 The difference between "animism" and "totemism" is, in this regard, *pace* Descola and with Sahlins, not very clear and pos-sibly not very meaningful. See Descola (2013), Sahlins (2014).

11 If a human being (in this self-referential sense) starts seeing a being of another species as human, this means that the first is in

the process of abandoning its position of subject and of turning into the potential prey of the other, become subject-predator.

12 The question of knowing whether *animals* know that *we* know it is the object of some controversy among ethnographers and of a possible cultural variation among different indigenous groups.

13 But not, it should be noted, in several of those philosophies that Meillassoux (2012) calls "subjectalist."

14 "Kwakiutl consider the human substance the standard for all life. In postulating a human-based consubstantiality they do not however convert the animal world into a Disneyland of mock characters. They attribute to animals speech, concern for interchange, and Winter Ceremonials – but also distinct and secret lifes" (Goldman 1975: 208).

15 As Alexandre Nodari reminds us, Latour's "being-qua-other" is something like the metaphysical expression of Oswald de Andrade's anthropophagic aphorism, "I am only interested in what is not mine." There would be much more to be said about the ontology of difference that would allow us to connect Andrade's speculations on the "matriarchate of Pindorama," the Amerindian thought of immanent otherness, and some contemporary philosophical and anthropological developments, among which Latour's own project (see Viveiros de Castro 2014).

16 See Jensen (2013).

17 The beings from the absolute "past" described in the myth, like spirits, the Masters of animals, deities and other usually invisible entities that compose the intentional substrate of the world are imperishable (Pierri 2014a), and therefore omni*present*, in the spatial as well as the temporal sense.

18 Death is the foundation, in the sense of *reason*, of the "economy of symbolic exchange" (Baudrillard 1976) of the Yanomami. This argument is fully developed in Albert's (1993) seminal article about the "shamanic critique of the political economy of nature" contained in Davi Kopenawa's discourse, which includes a sarcastic appraisal of the Whites' fetishism of the commodity, as well as its intrinsic relation to cannibalism.

19 Dreams, particularly shamanic dreams induced by the consumption of hallucinogenics, are the royal road to knowing the invisible foundations of the world, for the Yanomami as well as various other Amerindian peoples. See Viveiros de Castro (2007).

20 Just as Marx borrowed from the colonialist imaginary the term "fetishism," thus (re)opening, perhaps inadvertently, a rich analytical vein regarding the deep relations between economy and theology in Western metaphysics.

21 "What they [Whites] call 'nature' is, in our very ancient language *urihi a*, the forest-land" (Kopenawa and Albert 2013: 514). Compare this to Ursula Le Guin's beautiful *The Word for World is Forest* (2010: 105–6): "He had also come to like the Athsheans names for their own lands and places, sonorous two-syllabled words: Sornol, Tuntar, Eshreth, Eshsen that was now Centralville, Endtor, Abtan, and above all Athshe, which meant the Forest, and the World. So earth, terra, tellus meant both the soil and the planet, two meanings and one. But to the Athsheans soil, ground, earth was not that to which the dead return and by which the living live: the substance of their world was not earth, but forest. Terran man was clay, red dust. Athshean man was branch and root."

22 We do not intend here to speculate on the reasons for this "pre-science" of non-modern peoples, which little by little has left the domain of edifying allegories to take on a disturbing ecological literality. But among them we could certainly count the multi-millenial reflexive apprehension by the "savage mind" of certain constants of great generality in experience – constants which in the nineteenth century we have learnt to call thermodynamic, the "forgetting" of which lies at the root of the economic mutations that have taken place through successive crisis throughout the West's history. ("Economy" here should be understood in all its connotations, from accounting to theology.) We should of course not discard a tendency of human mythopoietical imagination towards a circular or recombinatory character in what regards time as well as space.

23 Some humans of the first Earth, by virtue of their antisocial behavior (which anticipates the *habitus* of the future animal) were transformed into animals of the present Earth (without, however, losing their imperishable anthropomorphic images, which inhabit the celestial layer); others, on the contrary, have attained a degree of "maturity" or "perfection" that made them identical to celestial deities. For a detailed discussion of Guarani eschatologies, particularly the Mbyá's, see Pierri (2013, 2014b).

24 For a dated but still useful survey of cosmogonies and eschatologies of indigenous South American, see Sullivan (1988).

25 These myths did not fail to "always have predicted" this return (Lévi-Strauss 1996). In other variants, Whites went away because of an error of judgment of Indians themselves, who foolishly sent them away or let them leave carrying with them all the instruments of their future technological prowess.

26 See, for example, Mesquita (2013), Hammer (2014), and Macedo (n.d.).

27 Translator's note: the reference here, which is immediately evident to a Brazilian reader, is to the "Program for the Acceleration of Growth" (*Programa de Aceleração do Crescimento*, or PAC), a major public-private partnership infrastructure development program initiated during Luis Inácio Lula da Silva's second term as Brazilian president, from 2006 to 2009. It was directed by his chief of staff, and later successor, Dilma Rousseff.

28 This brings to mind an episode in the Guarani myth of creation, in which the mythical twins exterminate (by drowning) the entire population of cannibal jaguars that dominated the Earth, but allow a pregnant female to escape which will then originate presently existing jaguars – thankfully less numerous than their originary archetypes.

29 Litaiff (1996: 116), cited in Pierri (2013).

Chapter 7 Humans and Terrans in the Gaia War

1 Anders' writings, as we have seen, sought to extract the implication of humankind's entrance into the Atomic Age, but they have plenty of lessons for our fall into the Anthropocene, given the density of the relation, both epistemological (Masco 2010, 2012) and ontological, between these two temporal milestones.

2 See Shryock and Smail (2011), Brooke (2014).

3 Even though the American way of life remains the undisputed champion when it comes to per capita greenhouse gas emissions, China has overtaken the United States in becoming the world's greatest producer of carbon dioxide in absolute terms. See Anderson and Bows (2011) for a desolating projection of the increase in global temperatures in a scenario taking into account the rapid growth of emissions in countries like China and India. The two authors show that, taking these into account, reduction goals set for so-called Annex I countries (notionally the most developed) in United Nations climate negotiations are irrisory and unable to prevent a rise in temperature well above 2°C – a limit which, incidentally, is far from being "safe," as was once thought. In the world scene, Brazil still reaps the credit acquired with the reduction of emissions caused by deforestation in the period between 2004 and 2012; however, apart from deforestation having started to climb up again since 2013, emissions coming from the energy sector have been growing in relative importance. Note to the English edition: The Paris Agreement

does not mention Annex I and Annex II countries, referring to developing and least developed countries.

4 Edmund Wilson, the famous entomologist, father of sociobiology and today an activist in the struggle against global warming, might be considered one of the high priests of the cult, discussed by Latour (2013d) in the first of his Gifford Lectures, of an "epistemological Nature" defined by the attributes of exteriority, unicity, de-animation, and indisputability.

5 One is reminded here of the opening paragraph in the "second phase" of *Livro do Desassossego*, by Bernardo Soares (Fernando Pessoa), where we can read the following meditation: "It occurred to me that God, being improbable, could exist; and so could be something that we should worship; but Humankind, being no more than a biological idea, meaning no more than the Human animal species, was no worthier of worship than any other animal species" (Pessoa 2013: 225).

6 Of great pertinence to this discussion is a recent piece by Idelber Avelar (2013), in which the author sets up a dialogue between the cosmopolitical aporias of the Anthropocene (following Chakrabarty) and Amerindian perspectives.

7 Translator's note: "humankind of reference" and "ethnos of reference" should be understood in the context of Viveiros de Castro's proposed solution to the apparent antinomy between the so-called "animism" of indigenous peoples (which extends humanity to all beings) and their "ethnocentrism" (which denies humanity to all outside the group): Amerindian perspectivism entails that each being/collective conceives itself as human from its *own* perspective – thus constituting a "humankind of reference" that establishes the criteria according to which humanity can be extended or denied to others. For the classic statement of that thesis, see Viveiros de Castro (1998).

8 Think of the theonomastic "tables of translation" discussed by Jan Assmann in relation to the ancient Middle East, evoked by Latour (2013d) in the first of his Gifford Lectures. It is curious, we should note, that, when discussing the phenomenological vacuity of the concept of species, Chakrabarty makes no reference to the concept of *Gattungswesen* deployed by Marx in the 1844 *Manuscripts* – which did not fail, back in the good old days, to generate heated debates within Marxism. Translated into English as "species being," it is known in Portuguese as "*essência genérica*," that is, generic (hence universal) essence.

9 Taking note of the insufficiency of critical sociology in no way entails, for Chakrabarty, that the latter is superfluous, let alone wrong-headed. It cannot be argued, however, that such a diagnosis implies an ideological jolt, not to say a narcissistic wound,

to the several strains of the left that claim faithfulness to historical materialism, since the problem with the sociology of globalization would ultimately be precisely its lack of materialism and its narrow historical provincialism. For a stimulating critique of the recent use of the notion of "human species" or "humankind" as agent of environmental collapse that seeks to circumvent economistic simplism, see Bonneuil and Fressoz (2016).

10 "From the present perspective of total catastrophe, Marx and Paul seem to have become contemporaries" (Anders 2007: 92).

11 See note 8 of this chapter, above.

12 It would not be absurd to argue that the image of humanity as a single, universal essence had ceased to make *metaphysical* sense since the Nazi program of systematic extermination of Jews, hence before Hiroshima. If total nuclear war entails the end of humankind "by means" of the end of the world, the Shoah means the end of "the world of humankind," the humanist European world that began in the Renaissance. The end of humankind, in that sense, began in Auschwitz, as much as the end of its future began in Hiroshima.

13 As in the vast majority of anti-nuclear discourse from the Cold War period, Anders' text proceeds as if humans were the only species whose extinction was at stake in the prospect of nuclear holocaust. See Danowski (2012a).

14 On top of having forced cattle into cannibalism – see Lévi-Strauss (2001).

15 This did not prevent Anders (Ibid.: 39–40) from highlighting a certain grey zone in the line dividing the two "humankinds," since, in the case of the atomic race, the fact of having the bomb made a country as, if not more, internally unsafe as those who did not have it, as that made it into a priority target for other atomic powers. In the case of the Anthropocene, on the other hand, the inequality in conditions is, at least at first, much clearer – the countries that contribute the most to global warming are those that find themselves, temporarily at least, in the safest position, owing to their capacity for economic mitigation of the devastating effects of climate change on their own territories.

16 Among some Amerindian peoples, bad dreams must be publicly narrated upon waking up so that the events prefigured in them will not come true.

17 We should note in passing that Latour himself (2011b, 2013a) has resorted to Hamilton's argument that, for as long as we do not abandon all hope, we will do nothing. We should also recall Steven Shapin's (2014: 29) rebuttal to Chomsky's exhortation to

optimism: "pessimism about the nature, scope and seriousness of our problems can be far more productive than complacent optimism. If necessity is the mother of invention, fear is its grandmother. Be afraid." For an eloquent, non-Pollyanna-esque defense of hope as a political principle, see, on the other hand, Rebecca Solnit's (2004) beautiful book.

18 The triad *demos*, *theos* and *nomos* structures the exposition of the "political theology of nature" advanced in Latour (2013a).

19 Although we should also bear in mind that the atemporality and universality of these laws are equally open to discussion nowadays; see, for example, the work of Lee Smolin, who partially takes up Peircean ideas (which are also, even if the author might not realize it, Tardean and Nietzschean) on the historicity of cosmic forces. See Povinelli (2013).

20 See also Latour (2011b), where the sublunary/supralunary distinction makes its first appearance, derived perhaps from Peter Sloterdjik's *Spheres* series.

21 It is precisely because it is not a work of architecture or engineering that Gaia cannot be re-engineered either (Latour 2013a: 66), which suggests that the author does not harbor great hopes in relation to climate geoengineering projects.

22 Gaia would be, so to speak, the agent of a *geostory* rather than the patient of a *geohistory*.

23 Even people who accept this consensus, Latour (2013a) points out, often do not feel capable of doing anything immediate and concrete that could help us escape the catastrophe. We are practical denialists in our comfortable or fatalistic quietism, he concludes in consternation, speaking for many though not, it should be said, for all.

24 See Shapin (2014: 29) on the perennial debate surrounding Malthus' thesis: "Malthusian debates belong to scientific inquiry, but it's an inquiry that is itself embedded within ongoing moral conversations – and we rarely expect consensus to emerge from those."

25 The above passage is, if memory does not fail us, the most trenchant expression of radicality and engagement on the part of Latour, who remains somewhat ambivalent as regards his own position in this war between two worlds. Although he has declared (or confessed) himself several times as a diplomat representing the Moderns, it is not hard to see that the author has tended more and more in the opposite direction, seemingly wishing to act, as Alyne Costa (2014) has remarked, "as a Terran infiltrated among Humans," whose mission would be to convert them and eventually help them to come round to the side of the people of Gaia.

26 The terms "key" and "mode of extension" make reference here to the vocabulary of *An Inquiry into Modes of Existence.*

27 Translator's note: an untranslatable play on the fact that, in Latin languages, the same word (*tempo, tiempo, temps*) can be used to say both "time" and "weather."

28 We refer the reader back to the prefatory note, in which we discuss our choice of "Terrans" (rather than "Earthlings" or "Earthbound people," the terms that Latour himself employs in his Gifford Lectures) to translate the French "*Terriens.*"

29 The horse in the title, a key character, disappears as Terran from Latour's analysis, as Juliana Fausto (2013) points out.

30 See Wagner (1981: 89) on the "dullness that we find in mission schools, refugee camps, and sometimes in 'acculturated' villages."

31 The book is a Nietzschean "anti-Bible," the director explains (Tarr 2011).

32 "The territory is German, the Earth Greek" (Deleuze and Guattari 1987: 339).

33 The approximation between Terrans and Deleuze and Guattari's "people that is missing" was suggested to us by Juliana Fausto (2013). Alexandre Nodari, on the other hand, has reminded us of the passage in Clarice Lispector's (2011: 102) *The Hour of the Star* in which the main character, Macabéa, is described as belonging to "a stubborn race of dwarves that one day might reclaim the right to scream."

34 "[T]his 'anthropos' whose civilization is already powered by around 12 terawatts (1012 watts), and which is heading toward 100 terawatts if the rest of the world develops at the level of the US, a stunning figure if one considers that plate tectonic forces are said to develop no more than 40 terawatts of energy" (Latour 2013a: 76). In fact, several sources indicate an even higher global consumption than that (around 15 TW), and the United States of America, where only 5 percent of the global population live, is responsible for 26 percent of that total amount.

35 We can do no better here than recommend the sharp critique to which Marilyn Strathern (2004) has subjected the Latourian notion of the moderns' "long networks," as well as the same author's reflection on scalarity as an instrument (and/or effect) of anthropological theory rather than as a property of phenomena observable, so to speak, to the naked eye.

36 See also Vidal (2003) and the eloquent images in Catraca Livre (2014).

37 Translator's note: Spanish in the original. "Good living" (*vivir bien*, in Spanish; *suma qamaña*, in Aymara; *sumak kawsay*, in Quechua; *teko porã*, in Guarani) is a concept common to various indigenous peoples of South America that gained political and

international currency over a decade ago as a consequence of the rise of left-leaning, indigenous-supported governments in the region.

38 We thank Alexandre Nodari for his clarifications regarding the Schmittian notion of the modern *nomos* or partition of the Earth, inaugurated with the invasion of America and India, then terminated (always according to Schmitt) with the rise of the United States and the creation of the League of Nations. Nodari suggests that the contemporary *nomos* would be something like the division between "legitimate" nation states and "rogue states" or the Axis of Evil (to which we could add "vandals," *casseurs*, Black Blocs, Zapatistas, the people up in arms etc.); and that a future *nomos* would emerge from the catastrophic scenario imagined by Isabelle Stengers, in which a world state would exercise its universal domination authorized to intervene wherever, whenever and however by the "urgency" (exception) of environmental collapse.

39 A statement, we dare say, that marks a veritable tipping point in Latour's worldview.

40 See Latour's (2013a: 95) statement about the idea of loop being constitutive of "what it means to be 'of this Earth'."

41 This project has also been given the name of "intensive sufficiency" (Viveiros de Castro 2011b).

42 For the idea of "uncivilization," see The Dark Mountain Project (2009).

43 In the language advanced in *An Inquiry into Modes of Existence*, Latour would classify these examples as so many cases of the crossing between the technology (TEC) mode of existence with several other modes of existence (REP, ORG, POL etc.). We have no objection to make to that.

44 Translator's note: the link containing this passage is only available to registered uses of the AIME website (<http://modesofexistence.org/>).

45 Translator's note: the paragraph alludes to and cites the 1977 song "*Um Índio*" ["An Indian"], by Brazilian singer-songwriter Caetano Veloso.

46 The REP-TEC distinction in *An Inquiry* ultimately strikes us as evidence of a certain anthropocentrism of Moderns; as is, in fact – nor could it be otherwise – the whole ontology of Moderns described by that book, despite it being presented in a reconstructed, pluralized version by Latour. Upon examining the table at the end of the book containing the fifteen modes of existence analyzed therein, we could not help but notice that it seemed as if – to paraphrase another well-known philosopher – animals and other beings are "mode of existence-poor," whereas

humans (and Moderns in particular) appear as eminently "mode of existence-forming."

47 We are following Latour here. But one does not need Schmitt to know what a political enemy is.

48 Who says history does not go back? See Walsh (2014) and the equally, if not even more troubling article by Peeples (2014).

49 See Clark (2013). For a more recent list of the 200 main state companies classified according to the potential carbon emissions of their declared fossil fuel reserves, see Fossil Free Indexes (2015). See also the *Carbon Tracker Initiative* website: <http://www.carbontracker.org/site/>.

50 See ETC Group (2008), Food Processing (2015).

51 An overview of the still heated debate concerning the extent of the invasion of the Americas' demographic can be found in Mann's (2005) well-documented book.

52 Translator's note: The authors make an untranslatable play here on the sound of the words "Melancolia" [*melancholia*] and "mercadoria" [*commodity*] in Portuguese.

53 See International Union For Conservation of Nature (2009), as well as the previously mentioned Elizabeth Kolbert (2014), and David Ulansey's staggering *The Current Mass Extinction* website (<http://www.mysterium.com/extinction.html>), which accumulates news on the current mass extinction since 1998.

54 Or maybe the Mayan collapse was that one thing which may be even less thinkable than the end of the world: the end of a state, *the end of the State*, with which the peoples submitted to it recover their self-determination? If every document of culture, as Walter Benjamin reminded us, is equally a document of barbarism, this applies just as much to the great works, monuments and knowledges produced by Mesoamerican and Andean civilizations.

55 Here is what the great theoretician of the modern *nomos* of the Earth had to say about this process: "The intellectual advantage [*geistige Überlegenheit*, which would just as easily be translated as 'spiritual superiority'] was entirely on the European side, so much so that the New World simply could be 'taken'" (Schmitt 2006: 132). Could this be an echo of Hegel's (1956: 81) perverse formulation, according to which American culture was destined to "expire as soon as Spirit approached it"?

Conclusion: World on the brink

1 Gaia has also been one of Latour's concerns since at least 2010 (see Latour 2010b).

2 It is true that, as the *theos* of the new cosmological assemblage under whose flag the people that is missing must march into war against Humans, Latour's Gaia could also be described as an operation.

3 We are extrapolating here from a brief allusion in Latour (2013d: 9).

4 The same happens when it is read by an innovative analytical philosopher such as Galen Strawson (see Strawson et al. 2006), whose consistent defense of panpsychism as a necessary corollary of "physicalist realism" has kept several champions of materialism busy – much to the amusement of those anthropologists who have tried for years to make academic philosophy take animism and panpsychism seriously, that is, to retrieve them back from the dustbin of the history of philosophy and accept them as metaphysical positions big with future: as prospective more than retrospective ideas.

5 Such themes, that of hesitation in particular, bring the two of them close to an anthropologist like Marilyn Strathern; we could call them the ethico-affective correlate of the operation of "ontological delegation" as defined by Gildas Salmon (2013) in a brilliant intervention at the Colloque de Cérisy on "Comparative Metaphysics."

6 We refer to this as the "first" manifesto as there is a new version, which nevertheless rehashes the same points; see Srnicek, Williams and Avanessian 2014.

7 See Beller (2006) on the "cinematic mode of production."

8 Against the bricolages of the savage thinker, which operates with whatever is at hand, tirelessly resignifying the world from within the limits of the actually existing world, the accelerationist political engineer (who is unlikely to hesitate in the face of the fabulous promises of geo-engineering proper) intends to create an ideal world through the rational power of the concept. We can thus see what is at stake in this confrontation; see Lévi-Strauss (1966).

9 Note that we are not asking whether these things will happen, because they are already happening. We only ask when they will become so evident that future futurological manifestos will have to be, so to speak, more attentive to their present.

10 The disabused admission of the "fetishistic" character of democratic liberties suggests that their suspension is seen as a condition for "political action" that will enable *Homo sapiens* to expand "beyond the limitations of the earth and our immediate bodily forms" [*sic*] (Williams and Srnicek 2013). The impression one is left with is that the authors can barely disguise their

metaphysical terror in the face of the species' terrestrial, mortal condition under the cover of an almost hysterical, authoritarian optimism.

11 See Philippe Bihouix for a well-argued critique of the oft-repeated idea that an ever greater refinement of "cutting edge" (or "high") technology could come to our rescue in the environmental crisis. The author proposes rather the "iconoclastic" thesis that we urgently need to orient ourselves "towards a society...based on low technologies, no doubt less pliable and more basic, perhaps a little less efficient, but patently more resource-efficient and locally controllable" (Bihouix 2014: 10). That cannot fail to bring to mind Oswald de Andrade's remark on Anthropophagy being "the only system fit for survival when the world runs out of writing ink."

12 See Pignarre and Stengers (2011) on "capitalist sorcery."

13 The growing use of non-polluting or "renewable" energies – aeolic, solar, tidal, as well as the much more controversial use of hydroelectricity obtained through the damming of rivers (with the large scale deforestation and displacement of populations that this entails), the conversion of agricultural areas for the production of biofuels, not to mention nuclear energy – has so far been, sadly but predictably, a supplement rather than a substitute for greenhouse gas-producing fossil fuel. Fracking and offshore drilling (soon in the Arctic as well) expand everywhere full speed ahead at the same time as ambitious solar and aeolic energy projects soldier on. And even if it is unlikely that the geo-engineering projects that have been conceived thus far will ever come to work – in the sense of stabilizing the climate system – let alone work without causing massive collateral damage, the sheer idea of them may, for as long as they remain in the cards as a plan B in international negotiations, contribute to arguments in favor of maintaining the present pattern of CO_2 emissions. See Tanuro (2016).

14 See Gaston (2013: 132): "Warning against the temptation to treat this cohabiting world as a simple unity or loss of difference, Derrida insists that one cannot truly establish that 'the world is one and the same thing' for two human beings let alone animals and humans. Within the cohabiting world, Derrida will argue, there is always more than one world."

15 For a very real retreat, see Plumer (2014).

16 Winnicott's brilliant lesson concerning the "good enough mother" (the mother that is good enough to raise a normal child – if she is "too good," the child will not turn out normal enough) seems not to have reached the ears of those who fret

over the kind of world we can live and will be capable of living in. For the idea of "intensive sufficiency," see Viveiros de Castro (2011b) and Anne Ryan (2009).

17 Translator's note: "Aldeia Maracanã" [Maracanã Village] was the name by which the occupation of an abandoned public building in Rio de Janeiro evicted in 2013 became known. The crumbling nineteenth-century palace, next door to the iconic Maracanã football stadium, had served as the headquarters of the first organ of the Brazilian government dedicated to indigenous policy and then as the Museum of the Indian [*Museu do Índio*]. Occupied by indigenous people in 2006, it was marked for demolition by the Rio de Janeiro state government in 2013, under the allegation (later denied) that this had been a condition imposed by FIFA for the 2014 World Cup. The occupiers' resistance catalyzed opposition to the state government and the socially damaging consequences of the World Cup, and the building became a place of convergence for indigenous people, activists and youth. Although the occupiers were finally evicted in March 2013, the process was widely recognized retrospectively as both an early sign of and an element that contributed to the explosion of discontent that produced the massive street protests of June 2013.

18 The traditional left, in alliance today with the elites that rule us, can only see (could only ever see) in the indigenous a kind of "poor": a future member of the working class destined to be emancipated. The time has come to see the "poor" from the structural position of the indigenous – after all, the ethnic matrix and a large part of the cultural unconscious of the poor population of Brazil are predominantly indigenous and African. This means that it is *not* a matter of liberating, improving, transforming them into a "less poor" version of ourselves, but to follow and to assist their self-determined transformation into something other than us, another people; the people, that is, that Darcy Ribeiro (2000) once so beautifully imagined as "the Brazilian people," a people to come if there ever was one, or if one ever became.

19 "[W]e must give the present the power to *resist the past*. This also means *revitalizing the past*, giving it the power to escape its classification as a part of the progressive history that leads to 'us'" (Stengers 2013b: 180; our emphasis). See also Strathern (1999: 246): "in certain respects 'traditional' Melanesian societies belong much more comfortably to some of the visions made possible by socioeconomic developments in Europe since the 1980s than they did to the worlds of the early and mid-twentieth century." Above all, see the powerful reflection taking

place around the political-metaphysical concept of Anthropoph-agy (including one of its components, the anthropologically subversive science of "Erratics"). Originally elaborated by the greatest philosophical name of Brazilian modernism, Oswald de Andrade, and currently being developed by the likes of Alexan-dre Nodari and other contemporary Latin American thinkers, this is a reflection upon which we unfortunately lack the space and time to expand here.

Bibliography

AAP (2013) "Climate Change Likened to Heat of Bomb Blasts." *The Sydney Morning Herald*, June 23. Available at: <http://www .smh.com.au/environment/climate-change/climate-change-likened -to-heat-of-bomb-blasts-20130622-2opo7.html>.

Abraham, John (2014) "Global Warming and the Vulnerability of Greenland's Ice Sheet." *Skeptical Science* blog, May 30. Available at: <http://www.skepticalscience.com/global-warming -vulnerability-greenland-ice-sheet.html>.

Albert, Bruce (1985) "Temps du Sang, Temps des Cendres: Représentation de la Maladie, Système Rituel et Espace Politique chez les Yanomami du Sud-Est (Amazonie Brésilienne)." Doctoral thesis, Université de Paris X (Nanterre).

Albert, Bruce (1988) "La Fumée du Métal: Histoire et Représentations du Contact chez les Yanomami (Brésil)." *L'Homme* 106–7, 28(2–3): 87–119.

Albert, Bruce (1993) "L'Or Cannibale et la Chute du Ciel. Une Critique Chamanique de l'Économie Politique de la Nature." *L'Homme* 126–8, 33(2–4): 349–78.

Almeida, Mauro William Barbosa de (2008) "A Fórmula Canônica do Mito." *Lévi-Strauss: Leituras Brasileiras*. Edited by Ruben Caixeta de Queiroz and Renarde Faria Nobre. Belo Horizonte: Editora da UFMG, 147–82.

Anders, Günther (2007) *Le Temps de la Fin*. Paris: L'Herne.

Anderson, Kevin, and Alice Bows (2011) "Beyond 'Dangerous' Climate Change: Emission Scenarios for a New World." *Philosophical Transactions of the Royal Society A*, 369: 20–44.

Available at: <http://rsta.royalsocietypublishing.org/content/369/1934/20.full>.

Andrade, Oswald de (1990) "A Crise da Filosofia Messiânica." *A Utopia Antropofágica*. São Paulo: Globo, 101–59.

Avelar, Idelber (2013) "Amerindian Perspectivism and Non-Human Rights." *Alter/nativas* 1: 1–21. Available at: <http://alternativas.osu.edu/en/issues/autumn-2013/essays/avelar.html>.

ASPTA (2013) "Encontro Nacional de Agricultoras e Agricultores Experimentadores Termina Celebrando a Partilha e a União." *ASPTA* website, November 1. Available at: <http://aspta.org.br/2013/11/3o-encontro-nacional-de-agricultoras-e-agricultores-experimentadores-termina-celebrando-a-partilha-e-a-uniao/>.

Badiou, Alain (2009) " 'L'Hypothèse Comuniste,' Interview à Pierre Gaultier." *Le Grand Soir*, August 6, 2009. Available at: <http://www.legrandsoir.info/L-hypothese-communiste-interview-d-Alain-Badiou-par-Pierre.html>.

Badiou, Alain, Thomas Bernatouil, Elie During, Patrice Maniglier, David Rabouin, and Jean-Pierre Zarander (2003) *Matrix: Machine Philosophique*. Paris: Ellipses.

Barnosky, Anthony et al. (2012) "Approaching a State Shift in Earth's Biosphere." *Nature* 486: 52–8.

Baudrillard, Jean (1976) *L'Échange Symbolique et la Mort*. Paris: Gallimard.

Beller, Jonathan (2006) *The Cinematic Mode of Production: Attention Economy and the Society of the Spectacle*. Lebanon, NH: Dartmouth College Press/University Press of New England.

Berardi, Franco (2009) *Precarious Rhapsody: Semiocapitalism and the Pathologies of the Post-Alpha Generation*. London: Minor Compositions.

Betts, Richard A., Matthew Collins, Deborah L. Hemming, Chris D. Jones, Jason A. Lowe, and Michael G. Sanderson (2011) "When Could Global Warming Reach 4°C?" *Philosophical Transactions of the Royal Society A*, 369: 67–84.

Bihouix, Philippe (2014) *L'Âge des Low Tech. Vers une Civilization Techniquement Soutenable*. Paris: Seuil.

Bonneuil, Christophe, and Jean-Baptiste Fressoz (2016) *The Shock of the Anthropocene: Earth, History and Us*. London: Verso.

Borges, Jorge Luis (2007) "Tlön, Uqbar, Orbis Tertius." *Labyrinths*. Translated by John M. Fein. New York: New Directions.

Brassier, Ray (2007) *Nihil Unbound: Enlightenment and Extinction*. New York: Palgrave MacMillan.

Brin, David (2012) *Existence*. London: Orbit.

Brook, Barry et al. (2013) "Does the Terrestrial Biosphere Have Planetary Tipping Points?" *Trends in Ecology & Evolution* 28/7: 396–401.

Brooke, John (2014) *Climate Change and the Course of Global History*. Cambridge: Cambridge University Press.

Bruckner, Pascal (2014) *The Fanaticism of the Apocalypse: Save the Earth, Punish Human Beings*. Cambridge: Polity.

Bryant, Levi, Nick Srnicek, and Graham Harman (eds.) (2011) *The Speculative Turn: Continental Materialism and Realism*. Melbourne: Re:press.

Butler, Octavia (2005) "Speech Sounds." *Bloodchild and Other Stories*. New York: Seven Stories Press, 87–110.

Calavia, Oscar (2001) "El Rastro de los Pecaríes. Variaciones Míticas, Variaciones Cosmológicas e Identidades Étnicas en la Etnología Pano." *Journal de la Société des Americanistes* 87: 161–76.

Calheiros, Orlando (2014) "Aikewara: Esboços de uma Sociocosmologia Tupi-Guarani." PhD thesis. Postgraduate Program in Social Anthropology, National Museum of Rio de Janeiro.

Carid, Miguel (1999) "Yawanawa: da Guerra à Festa." MA dissertation. Postgraduate Program in Social Anthropology, Federal University of Santa Catarina.

Catraca Livre (2014) "A Desigualdade Social no Mundo Captada em 6 Imagens Aéreas." *Catraca Livre* website, June 18. Available at: <https://catracalivre.com.br/geral/arquitetura/indicacao/a-desigualdade-social-pelo-mundo-captada-em-6-imagens-aereas/>.

CEPAT (2012) "Conjuntura da Semana. Gigantesco Retrocesso. Governo Cede a Ruralistas e 'Põe Fim' à Demarcação de Terras Indígenas." *Instituto Humanitas Online* website, s/d. Available at: <http://www.ihu.unisinos.br/cepat/cepat-conjuntura/520392-conjuntura-da-semana-gigantesco-retrocesso-governo-cede-a-ruralistas-e-poe-fim-a-demarcacao-de-terras-indigenas->.

Chakrabarty, Dipesh (2009) "The Climate of History: Four Theses." *Critical Inquiry* 35: 197–222.

Chakrabarty, Dipesh (2012) "Human Agency in the Anthropocene." *Perspectives on History* 50/9. Available at: <https://www.historians.org/publications-and-directories/perspectives-on-history/december-2012/the-future-of-the-discipline/human-agency-in-the-anthropocene>.

Chakrabarty, Dipesh (2014) "Climate and Capitalism: On Conjoined Histories." *Critical Inquiry* 42: 1–23.

Chery, Dady (2014) "Antarctica's Accelerating Ice Collapse." *Climate and Capitalism* website, May 30. Available at: <http://climateandcapitalism.com/2014/05/30/antarcticas-accelerating-ice-collapse/>.

Clark, Duncan, and KILN (2013) "Which Fossil Fuel Companies Are Most Responsible for Climate Change? – Interactive."

Guardian, November 20. Available at: <http://www.theguardian .com/environment/interactive/2013/nov/20/which-fossil-fuel -companies-responsible-climate-change-interactive>.

Coccia, Emanuele (2013) "Mente e Matéria ou a Vida das Plantas." *Landa* 1/2: 197–220. Available at: <http://www.revistalanda.ufsc .br/Edicoes/v1ed2-2013.html>.

Coetzee, J. M. (1999) *The Lives of Animals*. Princeton, NJ: Princeton University Press.

Coghlan, Andy, and Debora MacKenzie (2011) "Revealed: The Capitalist Network that Runs the World." *New Scientist* 24. Available at: <https://www.newscientist.com/article/mg21228354-500 -revealed-the-capitalist-network-that-runs-the-world/>.

Conklin, Beth (2001) *Consuming Grief: Compassionate Cannibalism in an Amazonian Society*. Austin, TX: Texas University Press.

Cook, John (2013a) "4 Hiroshima Bombs Worth of Heat per Second." *Skeptical Science* blog, July 1. Available at: <http:// www.skepticalscience.com/4-Hiroshima-bombs-worth-of-heat -per-second.html>.

Cook, John (2013b) "4 Hiroshima Bombs per Second: A Widget to Raise Awareness about Global Warming." *Skeptical Science* blog, November 25. Available at: <http://www.skepticalscience.com/ 4-Hiroshima-bombs-per-second-widget-raise-awareness-global -warming.html>.

Costa, Alyne de Castro (2014) "Guerra e Paz no Antropoceno: Uma Análise da Crise Ecológica segundo a Obra de Bruno Latour." MA dissertation. Philosophy Department, Pontifical Catholic University of Rio (PUC-Rio), Rio de Janeiro.

Craig, Amanda (2012) "The Hunger Games and the Teenage Craze for Dystopian Fiction." *Telegraph*, March 14. Available at: <http:// www.telegraph.co.uk/culture/books/9143409/The-Hunger -Games-and-the-teenage-craze-for-dystopian-fiction.html>.

Cronon, William (1995) *Uncommon Ground: Rethinking the Place in Nature*. New York: Norton.

Crutzen, Paul (2002) "Geology of Mankind." *Nature* 415: 23.

Crutzen, Paul, and Eugene Stoermer (2000) "The Anthropocene." *IGBP Newsletter* 41.

Curry, Patrick (2011) *Ecological Ethics: An Introduction*, 2nd edn, fully revised and expanded. Cambridge: Polity.

Danowski, Déborah (2001) "Indiferença, Simetria e Perfeição segundo Leibniz." *Kriterion* 42/104: 4971.

Danowski, Déborah (2011a) "David Hume, o Começo e o Fim." *Kriterion* 124: 331–43.

Danowski, Déborah (2011b) "Ordem e Desordem na *Teodicéia* de Leibniz." *Revista Índice* 3/1: 41–55.

Danowski, Déborah (2012a) "O Hiperrealismo das Mudancas Climáticas e as Várias Faces do Negacionismo." *Sopro* 70: 2–11. Available at: <http://www.culturaebarbarie.org/sopro/outros/hiperrealismo.html#.VvxQ7c4-Cu4>.

Danowski, Déborah (2012b). "καταστροφή: o Fim e o Começo." Paper presented at the colloquium *TerraTERRA* (People's Summit, Rio+20). Rio de Janeiro. Available at: <https://www.academia.edu/5071767/_o_fim_e_o_comeco>.

Davis, Mike (2006) *Planet of Slums*. London/New York: Verso.

Deleuze, Gilles (1990) *Logic of Sense*. Translated by Mark Lester with Charles Stivale. London: Athlone Press.

Deleuze, Gilles (1995) "Control and Becoming." *Negotiations 1977–1990*. Translated by Martin Joughin. New York: Columbia University Press, 169–76.

Deleuze, Gilles, and Félix Guattari (1987) *A Thousand Plateaus*. Translated by Brian Massumi. Minneapolis, MN: University of Minnesota Press.

Deleuze, Gilles, and Félix Guattari (1994) *What Is Philosophy?* Translated by Hugh Tomlinson and Graham Burchell. New York: Columbia University Press.

Derrida, Jacques (1984) "No Apocalypse, Not Now." *Diacritics* 14/2: 20–31.

Descola, Philippe (2013) *Beyond Nature and Culture*. Chicago, IL: Chicago University Press.

Dick, Philip K. (1983) *Ubik*. New York: Daw Books.

Domingos, João and Rafael Moraes Moura (2012) "Pessoas Contrárias a Hidrelétricas na Amazônia Vivem 'Fantasia', diz Dilma." *Estado de São Paulo*, April 5. Available at: <http://ciencia.estadao.com.br/noticias/geral,pessoas-contrarias-a-hidreletricas-na-amazonia-vivem-fantasia-diz-dilma,857484>.

Ennis, Paul (2013) "The Claim That We Are Already Dead." Unpublished manuscript.

ETC Group (2008) "Who Owns Nature? Corporate Power and the Final Frontier in the Commodification of Life." *ETC Group* website. Available at: <http://www.etcgroup.org/content/who-owns-nature>.

Evans-Pritchard, Edward (1939) "Nuer Time-Reckoning." *Journal of the International African Institute* 12/2: 189–216.

Farman, Abou (2012) "Re-Enchantment Cosmologies: Mastery and Obsolescence in an Intelligent Universe." *Anthropological Quarterly* 85/4: 1069–88.

Fasullo, John et al. (2013) "Australia's Unique Influence on Global Sea Level, 2010–2011." *Geophysical Science Letters* 40/16: 4368–73.

Fausto, Juliana (2013) "Terranos e Poetas: o 'Povo de Gaia' como 'Povo que Falta'." *Landa* 2/1: 165–81.

Fisher, Mark (2014) "Predator versus Avatar." *#Accelerate. The Accelerationist Reader*. Edited by Armen Avanessian and Robin Mackay. Falmouth/Berlin: Urbanomic/Merve, 335–46.

Foer, Jonathan Safran (2010) *Eating Animals*. London: Penguin.

Food Processing (2015) "Food Processing's Top 100." *Food Processing* website. Available at: <http://www.foodprocessing.com/top100/top-100-2013/>.

Fossil Free Indexes (2015) "The Carbon Underground. The World's Top 200 Public Companies Ranked by the Carbon Content of their Fossil Fuel Reserves." *Fossil Free Indexes* website. Available at: <http://fossilfreeindexes.com/research/the-carbon -underground/>.

Foucault, Michel (1973) *The Order of Things*. Translated by Alan Sheridan. New York: Vintage.

Freedman, Andrew (2013) "Australia's Flooding Rains Briefly Slowed Sea Level Rise." *Climate Central*, August 21. Available at: <http://www.climatecentral.org/news/floods-in-australia- briefly-slowed-sea-level-rise-study-finds-1637>.

Freedman, Andrew (2014) "Are We Totally Screwed? What Antarctica's 'Collapsing' Ice Sheet Means for Us." *Mashable*, May 20. Available at: <http://mashable.com/2014/05/20/antarctia -collapse-ice-sheet-how-worried/?utm_cid=mash-com-Tw-% 20main-link#DcW2bKL7caq2>.

Gabriel, Markus (2009) "The Mythological Being of Reflection." In Markus Gabriel and Slavoj Zizek, *Mythology, Madness, and Laughter: Subjectivity in German Idealism*. London: Continuum, 81–8.

Galinier, Jacques and Antoinette Molinié (2006) *Les néo-Indiens, une Religion du IIIeme Millénaire*. Paris: Odile Jacob.

Gallois, Dominique (1987) "O Discurso Waiãpi sobre o Ouro. Um Profetismo Moderno." *Revista de Antropologia* 30/31/32: 457–67.

Gaston, Sean (2013) *The Concept of World from Kant to Derrida*. London: Rowman & Littlefield.

Gerbi, Antonello (2010) *The New World Dispute: The History of a Polemic, 1750–1900*. Pittsburgh, PA: University of Pittsburgh Press.

Gil, Marie, and Patrice Maniglier (2015) *La Conversation des Images*. Paris: Bayard.

Goldman, Irving (1975) *The Mouth of Heaven: An Introduction to Kwakiutl Religious Thought*. New York: Wiley & Sons.

Hache, Émilie (ed.) (2014) *De l'Univers Clos au Monde Infini*. Bellevaux: Éditions Dehors.

Hache, Émilie, and Bruno Latour (2010) "Morality or Moralism? An Exercise in Sensitization." *Common Knowledge* 16: 311–30.

Hamilton, Clive (2010) *Requiem for a Species: Why We Resist the Truth about Climate Change.* Abingdon: Earthscan.

Hamilton, Clive (2012) "Love Your Scapegoats." *The Breakthrough Institute* website. Available at: <http://thebreakthrough.org/index.php/journal/letters-to-the-editor/love-your-scapegoats/>.

Hamilton, Clive (2014) "The New Environmentalism Will Lead Us to Disaster." *Scientific American*, June 19. Available at: <http://www.scientificamerican.com/article/the-new-environmentalism-will-lead-us-to-disaster/>.

Hammer, Patricia (2014) "Patsa Puqun: Ritual and Climate Change in the Andes." *ReVista. Harvard Review of Latin America*, Available at: <http://revista.drclas.harvard.edu/book/patsa-puqun>.

Hansen, James (2012) "Why I Must Speak Out About Climate Change." *TED* website. Available at: <http://www.ted.com/talks/james_hansen_why_i_must_speak_out_about_climate_change#t-453989>.

Hansen, James, Makiko Sato, and Reto Ruedy (2012) "The New Climate Dice: Public Perception of Climate Change." *National Aeronautics and Space Administration/Goddard Institute for Space Studies* website. Available at: <http://www.giss.nasa.gov/research/briefs/hansen_17>.

Hansen, James, et al. (2016) "Ice Melt, Sea Level Rise and Superstorms: Evidence from Paleoclimate Data, Climate Modeling, and Modern Observations that 2 °C Global Warming Could Be Dangerous." *Atmos. Chem. Phys.* 16: 3761–812.

Haraway, Donna (2013) "Cosmopolitical Critters, SF, and Multispecies Muddles." Paper presented at the *Gestes Spéculatifs* Colloquium, Centre Culturel International de Cérisy.

Hastrup, Kirsten (1990) "The Ethnographic Present: A Reinvention." *Cultural Anthropology* 5/1: 45–61.

Hegel, Georg Wilhelm Friedrich (1956) *The Philosophy of History.* Translated by C. J. Friedrich. New York: Dover.

Hunt, Terry, and Carl Lipo (2011) *The Statues that Walked: Unraveling the Mystery of Easter Island.* New York: Free Press.

International Union for Conservation of Nature (2009) "Extinction Crisis Continues Apace." *International Union for the Conservation of Nature* website, November 13. Available at: <http://www.iucn.org/?4143/Extinction-crisis-continues-apace>.

Israel, Brett (2010) "Study: Ocean Warmed Significantly Over Past 16 Years." *Live Science*, May 19. Available at: <http://www.livescience.com/6472-study-ocean-warmed-significantly-16-years.html>.

Jensen, Casper B. (2013) "Two Forms of the Outside: Castañeda, Blanchot, Ontology." *Hau – Journal of Ethnographic Theory* 3/3: 309–35. Available at: <http://www.haujournal.org/index.php/hau/article/view/122>.

Jonas, Hans (1985) *The Imperative of Responsibility: In search of an Ethics for the Technological Age*. Chicago, IL: University of Chicago Press.

Kingsnorth, Paul and Dougald Hine (2009) *The Dark Mountain Project Manifesto*. The Dark Mountain Project website, at: <http://dark-mountain.net/about/manifesto/>.

Kolbert, Elizabeth (2014) *The Sixth Extinction: An Unnatural History*. New York: Henry Holt & Co.

Kopenawa, Davi and Bruce Albert (2013) *The Falling Sky: Words of a Yanomami Shaman*. Cambridge, MA: Harvard University Press.

Koyré, Alexandre (2003) *Du Monde Clos à l'Univers Infini*. Paris: Gallimard.

Krøijer, Stine (2010) "Figurations of the Future: On the Form and Temporality of Protests Among Left Radical Activists in Northern Europe." *Social Analysis* 54/3: 139–52.

Krulwich, Robert (2013) "What Happened on Easter Island: A New (even Scarier) Scenario." *Krulwich Wonders* blog, *NPR* website, December 10. Available at: <http://www.npr.org/blogs/krulwich/2013/12/09/249728994/what-happened-on-easter-island-a-new-even-scarier-scenario>.

Kurzweil, Ray (2005) *The Singularity Is Near: When Humans Transcend Biology*. New York: Penguin.

Kurzweil, Ray (2009) "The Coming Singularity." *YouTube*. Available at: <https://www.youtube.com/watch?v=1uIzS1uCOcE>.

Land, Nick (2011) *Fanged Noumena: Collected Writings 1987–2007*. Windsor Quarry/New York: Urbanomic/Sequence.

Latour, Bruno (1993) *We Have Never Been Modern*. Translated by Catherine Porter. Cambridge, MA: Harvard University Press.

Latour, Bruno (2002) *War of the Worlds: What About Peace?* Chicago, IL: Prickly Paradigm Press.

Latour, Bruno (2008) "Le Fantôme de l'Esprit Public. Des Illusions de la Démocratie aux Réalités de Ses Apparitions." Introduction to Walter Lippmann. *Le Public Fantôme*. Paris: Editions Demopolis, 3–49.

Latour, Bruno (2010a) *On the Modern Cult of the Factish Gods*. Durham, NC: Duke University Press.

Latour, Bruno (2010b) "An Attempt at a 'Compositionist Manifesto'." *New Literary History* 41: 471–90.

Latour, Bruno (2011a) "Love Your Monsters." In Ted Norhaus and Michael Shellenberger, *Love Your Monsters:*

Postenvironmentalism and the Anthropocene. Oakland, CA: Breakthrough Institute, 17–25.

Latour, Bruno (2011b) "Waiting for Gaia: Composing the Common World Through Arts and Politics." Lecture at the Institut Français, London, November 21.

Latour, Bruno (2013a) *Facing Gaia: Six Lectures on the Political Theology of Nature. Being the Gifford Lectures on Natural Religion.* Lectures at Edinburgh University, February 18–28.

Latour, Bruno (2013b) "War and Peace in an Age of Ecological Conflicts." Lecture at the Peter Wall Institute, Vancouver, September 23.

Latour, Bruno (2013c) "Antropólogo Francês Bruno Latour Fala sobre Natureza e Política." Interview with Fernando Eichenberg. *O Globo*, December 28. Available at: <http://blogs.oglobo .globo.com/prosa/post/antropologo-frances-bruno-latour-fala-sobre -natureza-politica-519316.html>.

Latour, Bruno (2013d) *An Inquiry into Modes of Existence: An Anthropology of the Moderns.* Translated by Catherine Porter. Cambridge, MA: Harvard University Press.

Latour, Bruno (2015) *Face à Gaïa: Huit conférences sur le nouveau régime climatique.* Paris: Les Empêcheurs de Penser en Rond / La Découverte.

Le Guin, Ursula (2010) *The Word for World is Forest.* New York: Tor Books.

Leibniz, Gottfried W. (1990) *Theodicy: Essays on the Goodness of God, the Freedom of Man and the Origin of Evil.* Edited with an introduction by Austin Farrer. Translated by E. M. Huggard. Chicago, IL: Open Court.

Lévi-Strauss, Claude (1952) *Race and History.* Paris: UNESCO.

Lévi-Strauss, Claude (1961) *Tristes Tropiques.* Translated by John Russell. New York: Criterion Books.

Lévi-Strauss, Claude (1966) *The Savage Mind.* Translated by John and Doreen Weightman. Chicago, IL: University of Chicago Press.

Lévi-Strauss, Claude (1975) *The Raw and the Cooked. Mythologiques* volume 1. Translated by John Weightman and Doreen Weightman. New York: Harper & Row.

Lévi-Strauss, Claude (1988) *The Jealous Potter.* Translated by Bénédict Chorier. Chicago, IL: University of Chicago Press.

Lévi-Strauss, Claude (1996) *The Story of Lynx.* Translated by Catherine Tihanyi. Chicago, IL: University of Chicago Press.

Lévi-Strauss, Claude (2001) "La Leçon de Sagesse des Vaches Folles." *Études Rurales* 157–8: 9–14.

Lima, Tania S. (1996) "O Dois e Seu Múltiplo: Reflexões sobre o Perspectivismo em uma Cosmologia Tupi." *Mana* 2/2: 21–47.

Lima, Tania S. (2005) *Um Peixe Olhou para Mim: o Povo Yudjá e a Perspectiva*. São Paulo: Eduncsp/NuTI/ISA.

Lindblom, Jon (2012) "Techno-Cultural Acceleration. A Few Initial Remarks." Available at: <https://www.academia.edu/5686084/Techno-Cultural_Acceleration_A_Few_Initial_Remarks>.

Lispector, Clarice (2011) *The Hour of the Star*. Translated by Benjamin Moser. New York: New Directions.

Litaiff, Aldo (1996) *As Divinas Palavras. Identidade Étnica dos Guarani-Mbyá*. Florianópolis: UFSC.

Lyman, John et al. (2010) "Robust Warming of the Global Upper Ocean." *Nature* 465: 334–7.

McCarthy, Cormac (2006) *The Road*. New York: Vintage.

Macedo, Valéria (n.d.) "A Cosmopolítica das Mudanças (Climáticas e Outras)." *Instituto Socio-Ambiental* website. Available at: <http://pib.socioambiental.org/pt/c/no-brasil-atual/narrativas-indigenas/a-cosmopolitica-das-mudancas-%28climaticas-e-outras%29>.

Mackay, Robin (2012) "Nick Land – an Experiment in Inhumanism." *Umelec* 2012/1. Available at: <http://divus.cc/london/en/article/nick-land-ein-experiment-im-inhumanismus>.

MacKinnon, James Bernard (2013) *The Once and Future World: Nature As It Was, As It Is, As It Could Be*. New York: Houghton Mifflin Harcourt.

Mann, Charles (2005) *1491: New Revelations of the Americas Before Columbus*. New York: Vintage.

Mann, Michael (2012) *The Hockey Stick and the Climate Wars: Dispatches from the Front Lines*. New York: Columbia University Press.

Maranda, Pierre (ed.) (2001) *The Double Twist: From Ethnography to Morphodynamics*. Toronto: University of Toronto Press.

Masco, Joseph (2010) "Bad Weather: on Planetary Crisis." *Social Studies of Science* 40/1: 7–40.

Masco, Joseph (2012) "The End of Ends." *Anthropological Quarterly* 85/4: 1107–24.

Meillassoux, Quentin (2009) *After Finitude: An Essay on the Necessity of Contingence*. Translated by Ray Brassier. London: Bloomsbury.

Meillassoux, Quentin (2012) "Iteration, Reiteration, Repetition: A Speculative Analysis of the Meaningless Sign." Lecture at the Freie Universität, Berlin, April 20. Available at: <https://cdn.shopify.com/s/files/1/0069/6232/files/Meillassoux_Workshop_Berlin.pdf>.

Mesquita, Erika (2013) " 'Ver de Perto pra Contar de Certo.' As Mudanças Climáticas sob os Olhares dos Moradores da

Floresta." Doctoral thesis. Anthropology Department, University of Campinas.

Milton, John (2008) *Paradise Lost*. Oxford: Oxford University Press.

Monbiot, Georges (2014) "Destroyer of Worlds." *George Monbiot* website, March 24. Available at: <http://www.monbiot.com/2014/03/24/destroyer-of-worlds/>.

Morton, Timothy (2010) *The Ecological Thought*. Cambridge, MA: Harvard University Press.

Morton, Timothy (2013) *Hyperobjects: Philosophy and Ecology After the End of the World*. Minneapolis, MN: University of Minnesota Press.

Nimuendaju, Curt (1987) *As Lendas da Criação e Destruição do Mundo como Fundamentos da Religião dos Apapocúva-Guarani*. São Paulo: HUCITEC/EDUSP.

Nixon, Rob (2011) *Slow Violence and the Environmentalism of the Poor*. Cambridge, MA: Harvard University Press.

No REDD in Africa Network (2014) "Forced Relocation of Sengwer People Proves the Urgency of Cancelling REDD." *No REDD in Africa Network* website, March 12. Available at: <http://no-redd-africa.org/index.php/2-uncategorised/101-press-release-forced-relocation-of-sengwer-people-proves-urgency-of-canceling-redd>.

Nodari, Alexandre, and Flávia Cera. (2013) "A Horda Zumbi." *Rastros* 6: 1–4.

Nordhaus, Ted, and Michael Shellenberger (2009) *Break Through: Why We Can't Leave Saving the Planet to Environmentalists*. New York: Mariner Books.

Nordhaus, Ted, and Michael Shellenberger (2011) "The Long Death of Environmentalism." Lecture at the Yale School of Forestry and Environmental Studies, February 25. Available at: <http://thebreakthrough.org/archive/the_long_death_of_environmenta>.

Nordhaus, Ted, Michael Shellenberger, and Linus Blomqvist (2012) *The Planetary Boundary Hypothesis: A Review of the Evidence*. Oakland, CA: Breakthrough Institute.

Noys, Benjamin (2008) "Accelerationism." *No Useless Leniency* blog, October 20. Available at: <http://leniency.blogspot.com.br/2008/10/accelerationism.html>.

Noys, Benjamin (2012) "Cyberpunk Phuturism: The Politics of Acceleration." Talk given at the University of Brasília, October 1. Available at: <https://www.academia.edu/2197499/Cybernetic_Phuturism_The_Politics_of_Acceleration>.

Noys, Benjamin (2014) *Malign Velocities: Speed and Capitalism*. Winchester: Zero Books.

Nunes, Rodrigo (2014) "Ancestrality." *The Meillassoux Diction-ary*. Edited by Peter Gratton and Paul J. Ennis. Edinburgh: Edinburgh University Press, 22–4.

Ordnung, Alison (2013) "Touching on 12-12-13 at Kraupa-Tuskany Zeidler." *AQNB* website, December 23. Available at: <http://www.aqnb.com/2013/12/23/touching-on-14-12-13'-at-kraupa-tuskany-zeidler/>.

Oreskes, Naomi, and Erik M. Conway (2010) *Merchants of Doubt: How a Handful of Scientists Obscured the Truth on Issues from Tobacco Smoke to Global Warming*. New York: Bloomsbury Press.

Oreskes, Naomi, and Erik M. Conway (2014) *The Collapse of Western Civilization: A View from the Future*. New York: Columbia University Press.

Pálsson, Gisli, et al. (2013) "Reconceptualizing the 'Anthropos' in the Anthropocene: Integrating the Social Sciences and Humanities in Global Environmental Change Research." *Environmental Science & Policy* 28 (2013): 3–13.

Peeples, Lynn (2014) "The Stomach Bacteria That Could Prolong Your Life." *Huffington Post*, May 21. Available at: <http://www.huffingtonpost.com/2014/05/21/microbes-children-health_n_5366066.html?&ncid=tweetlnkushpmg00000048>.

Pessoa, Fernando (2013) *Livro do Desassossego*. Edited by Jerónimo Pizarro. Rio de Janeiro: Tinta-da-China.

Pierri, Daniel (2013) "Como Acabará Essa Terra? Reflexões sobre a Cataclismologia Guarani-Mbyá, à Luz da Obra de Nimuendaju." *Revista Tellus* 24.

Pierri, Daniel (2014a) "O Perecível e o Imperecível. Lógica do Sensível e Corporalidade no Pensamento Guarani-Mbyá." MA dissertation, Anthropology Department, University of São Paulo.

Pierri, Daniel (2014b) "O Dono da Figueira e a Origem de Jesus. Uma Crítica Xamânica ao Cristianismo." *Revista de Antropologia* 511: 265–301.

Pignarre, Philippe, and Isabelle Stengers (2011) *Capitalist Sorcery: Breaking the Spell*. Translated by Andrew Goffey. London: Palgrave Macmillan.

Plumer, Brad (2014) "Should We Try to Fight Rising Sea Levels – or Abandon the Coasts?" *Vox*, 9 July. Available at: <http://www.vox.com/2014/5/22/5735144/rising-sea-levels-abandoning-the-coasts>.

Povinelli, Elisabeth (2013) "Geontologies: Indigenous Worlds in the New Media and Late Liberalism." Lecture at the Colloquium *Métaphysiques Comparées*, Centre Culturel International de Cérisy, July–August 2013.

Ribeiro, Darcy (2000) *The Brazilian People: The Formation and Meaning of Brazil*. Gainesville, FL: University Press of Florida.

Rockström, Johan, et al. (2009) "A Safe Operating Space for Humanity". *Nature* 461: 472–5. Available at: <http://www.nature.com/nature/journal/v461/n7263/full/461472a.html>.

Ryan, Anne (2009) *Enough Is Plenty: Public and Private Policies for the 21st Century*. Winchester: Zero Books.

Sahlins, Marshall (2013) *What Kinship Is – and Is Not*. Chicago, IL: University of Chicago Press.

Sahlins, Marshall (2014) "On the Ontological Scheme of *Beyond Nature and Culture*." *HAU: Journal of Ethnographic Theory* 4/1: 281–90.

Salmon, Gildas (2013) "De la Délégation Ontologique: Naissance de l'Anthropologie Néo-Classique." Lecture presented at the Colloquium *Métaphysiques Comparées*, Centre Culturel International de Cérisy, July–August 2013.

Schieffelin, Edward (1976) *The Sorrow of the Lonely and the Burning of the Dancers*. New York: St. Martin's Press.

Schmitt, Carl (2006) *The* Nomos *of the Earth in the International Law of the* Jus Publicum Europaeum. Translated and annotated by G. L. Ulmen. New York: Telos Press.

Shapin, Steven (2014) "Libel on the Human Race." *London Review of Books* 36/11: 26–9.

Shaviro, Steven (2009) "Against Self-Organization." *The Pinocchio Theory* blog, May 26. Available at: <http://www.shaviro.com/Blog/?p=756>.

Shaviro, Steven (2011) "Panpsychism and/or Eliminativism." *The Pinocchio Theory* blog, October 4. Available at: <http://www.shaviro.com/Blog/?p=1012>.

Shaviro, Steven (2012) "Melancholia, or the romantic anti-sublime". *Sequence* 1.1. Available at: <http://reframe.sussex.ac.uk/sequence/files/2012/12/MELANCHOLIA-or-The-Romantic-Anti-Sublime-SEQUENCE-1.1-2012-Steven-Shaviro.pdf>.

Shryock, A., and D. L. Smail (2011) *Deep History: The Architecture of Past and Present*. Berkeley, CA: University of California Press.

Sloterdijk, Peter (2014) *Globes. Spheres, Volume 2: Macrospherology*. Translated by Wieland Hoban. Los Angeles, CA: Semiotext(e).

Sollin, Sverker and Paul Warde (eds.) (2011) *Nature's End: History and the Environment*. London: Palgrave MacMillan.

Solnit, Rebecca (2004) *Hope in the Dark: Untold Histories, Wild Possibilities*. New York: Nation Books.

Sonny, Julian (2013) "The Ten Things Technology Will Allow You to Do in the Next 50 Years." *Elite Daily* website, May

9. Available at: <http://elitedaily.com/news/technology/the-10-things-technology will allow-you-to-do-in-the-next-50-years>.

Srnicek, Nick, Alex Williams, and Armen Avanessian (2014) "#Accelerationism: Remembering the Future." *Critical Legal Thinking* blog, February 10. Available at: <http://criticallegalthinking.com/2014/02/10/accelerationism-remembering-future/>.

Steffen, Will et al. (2015) "Planetary Boundaries: Guiding Human Development on a Changing Planet." *Science* 347: 6223.

Stengers, Isabelle (2013a) "Matters of Cosmopolitics: Isabelle Stengers in Conversation with Heather Davis and Etienne Turpin on the Provocations of Gaïa." *Architecture in the Anthropocene: Encounters among Design, Deep Time, Science, and Philosophy.* Edited by Etienne Turpin. Ann Arbor, MI: Open Humanities Press, 171–82.

Stengers, Isabelle (2013b) *Une Autre Science Est Possible! Manifeste pour un Ralentissement des Sciences.* Paris: La Découverte.

Stengers, Isabelle (2015) *In Catastrophic Times: Resisting the Coming Barbarism.* Translated by Andrew Goffey. New Jersey: Open Humanities Press/Meson Press.

Sterzi, Eduardo (2009) "O Reino e o Deserto. A Inquietante Medievalidade do Moderno." *Letterature d'America (Brasiliana)* 29/125: 61–87. Available at: <https://periodicos.ufsc.br/index.php/nelic/article/view/26462>.

Stewart, George R. (1949) *Earth Abides.* New York: Ballantine Books.

Strathern, Marilyn (1999) *Property, Substance and Effect: Anthropological Essays on Persons and Things.* London: Athlone Press.

Strathern, Marilyn (2004) *Partial Connections.* Updated edition. Walnut Creek, CA: AltaMira Press.

Strawson, Galen, et al. (2006) *Consciousness and Its Place in Nature: Does Physicalism Entail Panpsychism?* Exeter/Charlottesville: Imprint Academic.

Sullivan, Lawrence Eugene (1988) *Icanchu's Drum: An Orientation to Meaning in South American Religions.* New York: Macmillan.

Szendy, Peter (2011) *Kant chez les Extraterrestres: Philosofictions Cosmopolitiques.* Paris: Minuit.

Szendy, Peter (2015) *Apocalypse-Cinema: 2012 and Other Ends of the World.* Translated by Will Bishop. New York: Fordham University Press.

Tanuro, Daniel (2016) "The Specter of Geoengineering Haunts the Paris Climate Agreement." *Climate and Capitalism*, January 25. Available at: <http://climateandcapitalism.com/2016/01/25/the-specter-of-geoengineering-haunts-the-paris-climate-agreement/>.

Tarde, Gabriel (1974) *Underground Man*. Translated by Cloudesley Brereton. Westport, CT: Hyperion.

Tarde, Gabriel (1980) *Fragment d'Histoire Future*. Paris: Slatkine.

Tarr, Béla (2011) Interview with Vladan Petkovic. *Cineuropa* website, March 4. Available at: <http://cineuropa.org/it.aspx?t =interview&lang=en&documentID=198131>.

United Nations Permanent Forum on Indigenous Issues (2009) "Who Are Indigenous Peoples?" *United Nations* website, n/d. <http://www.un.org/esa/socdev/unpfii/documents/5session _factsheet1.pdf>.

Valentine, David (2012) "Exit Strategy: Profit, Cosmology, and the Future of Humans in Space." *Anthropological Quarterly* 85/4: 1045–68.

Vidal, John (2003) "Every Third Person Will be a Slum Dweller within 30 Years, UN Agency Warns." *Guardian*, October 4. Available at: <http://www.theguardian.com/world/2003/oct/04/ population.johnvidal>.

Viveiros de Castro, Eduardo (1998) "Cosmological Deixis and Amerindian Perspectivism." *Journal of the Royal Anthropological Society* 4/3: 469–88.

Viveiros de Castro, Eduardo (2004). "Exchanging Perspectives: The Transformation of Objects into Subjects in Amerindian ontologies." *Common Knowledge* 10/3: 463–84.

Viveiros de Castro, Eduardo (2006) "No Brasil Todo Mundo é Índio Exceto Quem Não É." Instituto *Socio-Ambiental* website. Archived at: <http://pib.socioambiental.org/files/file/PIB_institucional/No _Brasil_todo_mundo_é_%C3%ADndio.pdf>.

Viveiros de Castro, Eduardo (2007) "The Crystal Forest: Notes on the Ontology of Amazonian Spirits." *Inner Asia* (Special Issue: Perspectivism) 9/2: 153–72.

Viveiros de Castro, Eduardo (2011a) "Zeno and the Art of Anthropology: of Lies, Beliefs, Paradoxes, and Other Truths." *Common Knowledge* 17/1: 128–45.

Viveiros de Castro, Eduardo (2011b) "Desenvolvimento Econômico e Reenvolvimento Cosmopolítico: da Necessidade Extensiva à Suficiência Intensiva." *Sopro* 51: 1–11. Available at: <http:// culturaebarbarie.org/sopro/outros/suficiencia.html>.

Viveiros de Castro, Eduardo (2012a) "Transformação na Antropologia, Transformação da Antropologia." *Mana* 18/1: 151–71.

Viveiros de Castro, Eduardo (2012b) *Cosmological Perspectivism in Amazonia and Elsewhere. Four Lectures Given in the Department of Social Anthropology, Cambridge University, February/*

March 1998. Hau Masterclass Series Volume 1. Available at: <http://www.haujournal.org/index.php/masterclass/issue/view/ Masterclass%20Volume%201>.

Viveiros de Castro, Eduardo (2014) *Cannibal Metaphysics*. Translated by Peter Skafish. Minneapolis, MN: Univocal.

Wagner, Roy (1981) *The Invention of Culture*, 2nd edn. Chicago, IL: University of Chicago Press.

Walsh, Bryan (2008) "Ted Nordhaus and Michael Shellenberger." *Time* magazine, September 24. Available at: <http://content.time.com/time/specials/packages/article/0,28804,1841778_1841779_1841804,00.html>.

Walsh, Fergus (2014) " 'Golden Age' of Antibiotics 'Set to End'." *BBC*, January 8. Available at: <http://www.bbc.com/news/health-25654112>.

Ward, Peter (2009) *The Medea Hypothesis: Is Life on Earth Ultimately Self-destructive?* Princeton, NJ: Princeton University Press, Book Club Edition.

Wark, McKenzie (2004) *A Hacker Manifesto*. Cambridge, MA: Harvard University Press.

Wark, McKenzie (2013) "#Celerity: a Critique of the Manifesto for an Accelerationist Politics." Available at: <http://speculativeheresy.wordpress.com/2013/05/14/celerity-a-critique-of-the-manifesto-for-an-accelerationist-politics/>.

Weisman, Alan (2007) *The World Without Us*. New York: Thomas Dunne/St. Martin's Press.

Weisman, Alan (2009) "The World Without Us." *AP04* website, April 6. Available at: <http://apo4.com/Science/TheWorldWithoutUs>.

Weisman, Alan (2013) "Crowded Planet. A Conversation with Alan Weisman." *Orion Magazine* website, October 22. Available at: <http://www.orionmagazine.org/index.php/articles/article/7694>.

Weiss, Gerald (1972) "Campa Cosmology." *Ethnology* 9/2: 157–72.

Weston, Jessie Laidlay (1920) *From Ritual to Romance*. Available at: <http://www.gutenberg.org/ebooks/4090>.

Whitehead, Alfred North (1979) *Process and Reality: An Essay in Cosmology*. New York: The Free Press /Macmillan.

Williams, Alex, and Nick Srnicek (2013) "#ACCELERATE. Manifesto for an Accelerationist Politics." *Critical Legal Thinking* website, May 14. Available at: <http://criticallegalthinking.com/2013/05/14/accelerate-manifesto-for-an-accelerationist-politics/>.

Williams, Evan Calder (2011) *Combined and Uneven Apocalypse: Luciferian Marxism*. Winchester: Zero Books.

Zeebe, Richard E., Andy Ridgwell, and James C. Zachos (2016) "Anthropogenic Carbon Release Rate Unprecedented during the Past 66 Million Years." *Nature Geoscience* 9: 325–9.

Zourabichvili, François (2012) *Deleuze: A Philosophy of the Event* together with *The Vocabulary of Deleuze*. Edited by Gregg Lambert and Daniel W. Smith. Translated by Kieran Aarons. Edinburgh: Edinburgh University Press.

Index